B-52
STRATOFORTRESS

The Complete History of the World's Longest Serving and Best Known Bomber

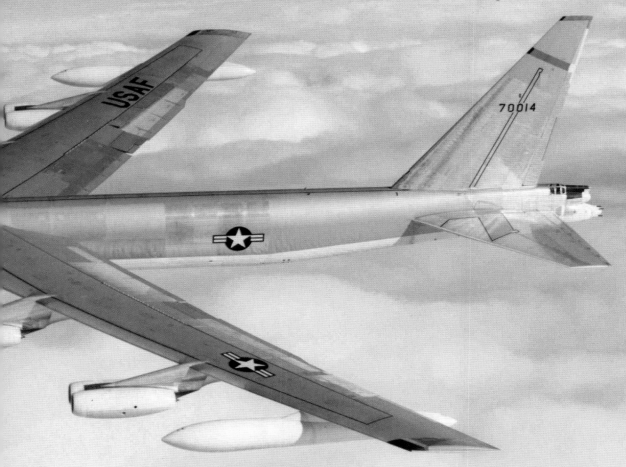

BILL YENNE

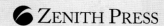
ZENITH PRESS

■ On the front cover:
A B-52H from the
20th Expeditionary
Bomb Squadron over
the Pacific Ocean
during the RIMPAC
exercise in July 2010.
*USAF photo, Tech. Sergeant
Jacob N. Bailey*

■ On the back cover:
Twenty-first century
flight deck: A B-52H
Stratofortress crew
prepares to take
fuel from a KC-135
Stratotanker. *USAF*

The fourth B-52G, to
be built at Wichita,
a Block 75 bird.

■ On the frontis:
The power elite
of the 1950s: A
Stratofortress draws
contrails across the
stratosphere. *USAF*

■ On the title page:
A Block 90 Seattle-
built B-52E prepares
to link up with a
KC-135.

First published in 2012 by Zenith Press, an imprint of MBI Publishing Company,
400 First Avenue North, Suite 300, Minneapolis, MN 55401 USA

© 2012 Zenith Press

Text © 2012 Bill Yenne

All photographs are from the author's collection unless noted otherwise.

Zenith Press titles are also available at discounts in bulk quantity for industrial or sales-promotional use. For details write to Special Sales Manager at MBI Publishing Company, 400 First Avenue North, Suite 300, Minneapolis, MN 55401 USA.

To find out more about our books, join us online at www.zenithpress.com.

Library of Congress Cataloging-in-Publication Data

Yenne, Bill, 1949-
 B-52 Stratofortress : the complete history of the world's longest serving and best known bomber / Bill Yenne.
    p. cm.
 Includes bibliographical references and index.
 Summary: "A comprehensive history of the B-52's development, manufacture, and combat service. The longest-serving U.S. Air Force combat aircraft, the B-52 debuted in 1955 and is slated to continue to 2040. It flew in the Cold War, Vietnam, the Gulf Wars, and Afghanistan"--Provided by publisher.
 ISBN 978-0-7603-4302-9
 1. B-52 bomber--History. 2. Air power--United States--History. I. Title.
 UG1242.B6Y46 2012
 358.4'283--dc23
                              2012025615

Editor: Scott Pearson
Design Manager: James Kegley
Designer: Diana Boger
Cover designer: Rob Johnson

Printed in China

10 9 8 7 6 5 4 3 2 1

Contents

Introduction: The Most Formidable Expression

THE BOEING B-52 STRATOFORTRESS is the ultimate embodiment of the principle of strategic air power and has been the cornerstone of American air power doctrine since well before the U.S. Air Force was formed out of the USAAF in 1947. It looked the part then, and it still does.

For this author, the first introduction to the powerful Stratofortress came as a young boy growing up on the northern tier of Montana, who used to lie on the lawn on warm summer evenings in the late 1950s and early 1960s staring up at the sky through a pair of high-powered binoculars.

The Stratofortresses came over, many thousands of feet above, their streaming contrails colored golden by the late rays of summer sun. Often they were in groups of three, and often they were attached to the booms of KC-135s. With the binoculars, the "U.S. Air Force" written on the forward fuselage was easily readable. Also clearly visible were the eight big Pratt & Whitney engines and the distinctive tall tails. The boy watched them until they disappeared over the trees and pondered the formidable power they represented. The boy watched them many times, perhaps dozens of times. The man into whom that boy grew has often wished he could go back and do it again, preferably with a camera and a 500mm lens.

Also burned into the memory of the boy who became a man is being half a mile from the end of the runway at Fairchild AFB, watching a minimum interval takeoff of Strategic Air Command B-52s. A whole squadron of the big bombers took off 12 to 15 seconds apart, their J57-P-29WA turbojets painting black contrails across the late afternoon sun.

The personal attachment of that boy who used to watch the Stratofortresses in the sky was cemented two decades later, when, as a man associated with the U.S. Air Force Art Program, he was afforded opportunities to go inside Stratofortresses from bases in the continental United States to Andersen AFB on Guam.

On June 25, 1980, he strapped himself into the jump seat on the flight deck of a 328th Bombardment Squadron B-52H, tail number 60-0051, at Castle AFB. The aircraft took off for a 12-hour mission that included aerial refueling over Pacific Ocean, a high-level simulated bombing run over the Nellis AFB test range, and the hair-raising and eye-opening experience of low-level operations over the 1st Combat Evaluation Group's Detachment 5 range near Wilder, Idaho. Down below, he glimpsed a farmhouse out of the corner of his eye and imagined another boy looking up.

Back in 1954, when the boy was first looking skyward at the sounds of airplanes and the Stratofortress was freshly accepted by the service, Secretary of the Air Force Donald

Making final flight line adjustments to a Pratt & Whitney J57 as Stratofortresses line up for delivery to the Strategic Air Command.

■ Above: It was at night, with the massive bombers bathed in the eerie light of mercury vapor lamps, that the Stratofortress best embodied their characterization as "the most formidable expression of air power in the history of military aviation."

■ Left: The eight throttle levers of a B-52D, with those for the numbers one and two engines—paired in the far port side nacelle—pushed forward. The Stratofortress is the only American jet bomber on which one would have found eight throttles. *Bill Yenne*

Quarles looked up at the immense aircraft and described it as "the most formidable expression of air power in the history of military aviation."

If he only could have known what was to come. Of all the words spoken, of all the attempts at being prophetic that have been heard at the rollouts of new aircraft and weapons systems, *none* have ever proven to be more accurate.

Within the American defense establishment, where an environment of concern over costs and cost overruns has been a daily reality for generations, it can be said that there is no other combat aircraft with which the American taxpayer got his or her money's worth to a greater extreme than with the Stratofortress.

Nor has any other combat aircraft ever remained in first-line service for so long. Even back in the 1990s, aviation historians commonly mentioned the axiom that the grandsons of the original B-52 crews were then serving aboard Stratofortresses.

The B-52 first entered service with the U.S. Air Force Strategic Air Command in the Cold War 1950s, where it would remain on alert until 1991 for the possibility of delivering immediate nuclear strikes at any time and any place in the world. During the 1960s and early 1970s, B-52s were flying conventional bombing missions against targets in Vietnam. In the 1990s, as the fleet was in its fourth decade of service, B-52s were flying conventional bombing missions against targets in Iraq and, later, in the Balkans. In 2001 and 2002, as these great warhorses were nearing their fiftieth anniversary, they were punishing al-Qaeda terrorists hiding in Afghan caves.

A B-52H from the 96th Expeditionary Bombardment Squadron takes off from Andersen AFB, Guam. *USAF photo, Senior Airman Christopher Bush*

■ A 5th Bombardment Wing B-52H Stratofortress on its approach to Minot AFB. *USAF photo, Sgt. Preston Chasteen*

The author during a June 1980 training mission aboard a B-52H, tail number 60-0051. *Bill Yenne*

In writing about a Cold War combat aircraft that had a subsequent career in Southeast Asia, one would be able to tell a significant story. To write about such an aircraft having a major role in Operation Desert Storm would add a great deal of richness to the tale. To add yet more layers across those five decades, reaching into a new century, would make such an airplane, in a word, *unique*. Yet, with the Stratofortress, the long and colorful career chronicled in this book is merely the *beginning*.

William Shakespeare, in Act 2 of *The Tempest*, penned the oft-repeated phrase "What's past is prologue," meaning that the past is merely the prelude to the present and to the future. The story of no aircraft in military history has ever been preceded by a prologue as extraordinary and as interesting as that of the Stratofortress.

Its legacy was assured long ago, but so, too, was its future.

A B-52H during an eight-hour practice bomb-dropping sortie on April 20, 2011. *USAF photo, Sgt. Andy Kin*

1

The Origins of Strategic
Air Power Doctrine

THE USE OF AIR POWER in warfare is said to date back to the first use of observation balloons by the French Aerostatic Corps at the Battle of Fleurus in 1794. During the Civil War, Abraham Lincoln became enamored with the concept and appointed balloonist Professor Thaddeus S. C. Lowe to serve as the U.S. Army's first chief aeronaut. The Union Army used observation balloons as early as 1861 at the time of the first Battle of Bull Run. The Confederates also later used balloons.

The use of fixed-wing aircraft in wartime, both as observation platforms and to drop bombs, is believed to have had its debut during Italy's 1911 operations in Libya against the crumbling Ottoman Empire. The technical establishment was slow to grasp the importance of such operations. In October 1910, *Scientific American* dismissed the idea of airplanes as war machines, noting that "outside of scouting duties, we are inclined to think that the field of usefulness of the aeroplane will be rather limited. Because of its small carrying capacity, and the necessity for its operating at great altitude, if it is to escape hostile fire, the amount of damage it will do by dropping explosives upon cities, forts, hostile camps, or bodies of troops in the field to say nothing of battleships at sea, will be so limited as to have no material effects on the issues of a campaign."

In the skies over World War I battlefields, first as observation platforms, then as war machines, this thesis was proven wrong. Air-to-air combat was a natural extension of the aircraft as an observation platform. Soon, aerial observers flying over the enemy's lines to observe realized that they could as easily drop something that exploded. Tactical bombing was born.

Tactical bombing, simply stated, is aerial bombardment of enemy targets, such as troop concentrations, airfields, entrenchments, and the like, as part of an integrated air-land battlefield action at or near the front. Tactical air power is generally used toward the same goals as, and in direct support of, naval forces or ground troops in the field.

Naturally, there were some far-sighted air power theorists who began imagining that aviation might potentially be deployed in such a way as to have "material effects" beyond the battlefield, thereby shaping the course and outcome of the war itself. This is what came to be known as *strategic* air power.

Strategic air power, in contrast to tactical air power, seeks targets without a specific connection with what is happening at the front. Strategic air power is used to strike far behind the lines at the enemy's means of waging war, such as factories, power plants, cities, and, ultimately, the enemy's very will to wage war. Strategic aircraft naturally differ from tactical aircraft in that they have a much longer range and payload capacity—certainly

A formation of U.S. Army Air Corps Keystone bombers over the Golden Gate on April 25, 1930, seven years before the famous bridge was built to span the entrance to San Francisco Bay. *U.S. Army*

The father of American air power, Gen. William Lendrum "Billy" Mitchell commanded the U.S. Army air component during World War I and afterward became an outspoken advocate of the potential of air power to win wars.

more than the average 1914 aeroplane. It was not until around the time of World War I that aviation technology had developed to the point where such aircraft were practical.

One of the original pioneers of strategic air power was a Russian engineer and aviation enthusiast named Igor Sikorsky, who would amaze the world 30 years later with the first practical helicopters. His 1913 aircraft, named Ilya Mourometz after the tenth-century Russian hero, was the world's first strategic bomber. In the winter of 1914–1915, a sizable number of these big bombers were in action against German targets. The payload of each bomber exceeded half a ton, and with a range of nearly 400 miles, they were able to hit targets well behind German lines. After initial victories, the Russian army was, by 1917, defeated on the ground; the Tsar had abdicated, and the events leading to the Russian Revolution were rapidly underway. The Ilya Mourometz had been successful in what it did, but it played only the tiniest part in one of mankind's biggest dramas.

Strategic air operations on the Western Front were soon to follow those in the east, with British aircraft launching strikes against German positions in occupied Belgian coastal cities in February 1915. The Germans countered with zeppelin attacks on Paris and on British cities as far north as Newcastle. By 1917, the Germans were using long-range, fixed-wing Gotha bombers against London. In April 1918, shortly after being established as an independent service, Britain's Royal Air Force (RAF) conducted a series of raids on German cities in the Ruhr and even ranged as far south as Frankfurt, though these raids were more strategic bombing experiments than a strategic bombing offensive. A full-scale strategic air offensive against Germany was scheduled for the spring of 1919, with Berlin on the target list, but the war ended in November 1918 with the plan untried.

Though the intervention of the United States manpower in World War I may have been of pivotal importance to the Allies, American involvement in the air war was not extensive. Nevertheless, strategic air power made an impression on the commander of the American Expeditionary Force (AEF) air units in the war, Col. William Lendrum "Billy" Mitchell. He became the first major American exponent of strategic airpower, but his ideas were never implemented during the war. Strategic bombing, though experimental in British and French doctrine, was not yet accepted by the American military establishment at all.

After the war, Mitchell argued that strategic bombers were cheaper to build and operate than battleships and that they could be used faster, and more easily, to project American power wherever it might be needed around the world. He raised hackles in 1921 when he told Congress that his bombers could sink any ship afloat. To prove him wrong, the Navy agreed to let him try out his theories on some German warships they had inherited at the end of the war that needed to be disposed of. They didn't think he could do it, but in July 1921, he proved them wrong, sinking several vessels, including

■ This picture is symbolic of the advent of air power as a weapon at a time when battleships were still the most formidable expression of a nation's military power.

In July 1921, Billy Mitchell's aircrews succeeded in sinking the captured German battleship *Ostfriesland*. The U.S. Navy was greatly embarrassed by this demonstration of the potential of air power to sink warships and tried to suppress the report of Mitchell's success. Many in the navy were in denial for 20 years—until Pearl Harbor. *U.S. Navy*

The British Royal Air Force Bomber Command, like the USAAF, demonstrated air power to the Third Reich—the hard way. Here we see an RAF Avro Lancaster over the inferno that was Hamburg, circa 1944.

A Keystone B-4A of the U.S. Army Air Corps 31st Bombardment Squadron (7th Bomb Group), seen on October 10, 1932, at Hamilton Field near San Francisco. *U.S. Army*

the heavily armored battleship *Ostfriesland*. Mitchell had dramatically proven his point, but both the U.S. Army and U.S. Navy remained officially unconvinced.

Mitchell's undoing was an unrelated incident in 1925, when, after the loss of life from the crash of the Navy dirigible *Shenandoah*, Mitchell called the management of national defense by the war and navy departments "incompetent" and "treasonable." Mitchell was court-martialed, convicted, and drummed out of the service on half pension. He died in 1936, just a few years short of seeing strategic air power play a key role in the Allied victory in World War II.

Nevertheless, even before the death of Billy Mitchell, the proponents of the still-unproven concept of strategic air power had risen to places of influence within the major air forces of the world. In both Britain and the United States, large, four-engine heavy bombers were in development, while in Germany, air power in general had been fully integrated into battlefield doctrine. When World War II began, the Germans stunned military planners everywhere with the effectiveness of their *blitzkrieg* ("lightning war") doctrine, in which tactical air power worked closely with rapidly moving mechanized ground forces.

Beginning in August 1940, the German Luftwaffe undertook the world's first major strategic air campaign, the Battle of Britain. The idea was to bring Britain to its knees solely through the use of an air assault on cities and industrial targets. The campaign ultimately failed, but there was no one who understood more how narrowly it failed than the strategic planners in the Royal Air Force. For them, and for the world, the Battle of Britain demonstrated the potential of strategic air power.

When the United States entered the war against Germany alongside Britain in 1941, a key element of Allied planning was a coordinated strategic air offensive against Germany. The creation of a large bomber force capable of a major air campaign against German industrial targets was a key objective of Allied planning in 1942. By 1943, enough aircraft were available for a Combined Bomber Offensive, which was formally begun in June 1943. Sustained air attacks against Germany were made on an almost daily basis by the RAF Bomber Command and the USAAF Eighth Air Force, operating from bases in England, and by the USAAF Fifteenth Air Force, operating from bases in Italy.

The stated objective, which provides a good definition of strategic air power, was "the progressive destruction and dislocation of the German military, industrial, and economic system, and the undermining of the morale of the German people to a point where their capacity for armed resistance is fatally weakened."

Billy Mitchell could have told them that, and in fact, he had.

■ By 1944, when the USAAF was mounting thousand-plane raids over Germany, there was no doubt of the commitment that military planners had made to the doctrine of strategic air power. *USAAF*

2

Boeing Bombers Before the Stratofortress

I N 1941, THERE WAS A BILLBOARD on East Marginal Way South in Seattle, Washington, that carried the slogan "Boeing Aircraft Company, World Center of 4-Engine Airplane Development." Pictured on this billboard were the Model 307 Stratoliner and the Model 314 Clipper, the transoceanic luxury flying boat that was then in service with Pan American. Leading the way in the picture was Boeing's Model 299 Flying Fortress, better known by its USAAF designation, B-17.

The slogan summarized what had happened across the street at Boeing Field. The company's Plant 2 had indeed become the "World Center of 4-Engine Airplane Development."

The actual road may have been East Marginal Way South, but the metaphorical road was the one that would lead to the B-52 Stratofortress.

This road had begun back in 1933, with two secret U.S. Army Air Corps programs that were called Project A and Project D. Two years later, these were merged as the Bomber, Long Range (BLR), program, which resulted in the Boeing XBLR-1. Redesignated as XB-15, the aircraft made its first flight in 1937 as the largest bomber yet built in America. However, the Air Corps had already moved on to requesting a smaller (though still large) and more modern aircraft. In response to this request, Boeing had proposed its Model 299, which had first flown in 1935, two years ahead of the XB-15.

■ Boeing's huge XB-15, the most massive airplane yet built in the United States, made its first flight in 1937. *National Archives*

■ This 1941 billboard, across from Boeing Field on East Marginal Way South, touted the company as the "World Center of 4-Engine Airplane Development." Left to right are the Model 307 Stratoliner, the Model 314 Clipper, and the B-17 Flying Fortress.

A classic image of USAAF B-17Fs high in the cold winter air, en route to Hitler's Germany. Boeing's Flying Fortress was the signature warplane in the massive strategic air offensive that helped defeat the Third Reich.

The Model 299 was designed by a team of brilliant young Boeing engineers, notably Edward Curtis Wells, and built at company expense. It first flew on July 28, 1935, powered by four Pratt & Whitney R1690 Hornet engines. At the rollout, a journalist described Boeing's huge, four-engine bomber as a "flying fortress." The nickname was quickly adopted as the official name. The Air Corps tested the Boeing-owned Model 299 under the unofficial XB-17 designation for nearly three months and ordered 13 service test Model 299B aircraft under the designation Y1B-17.

When World War II began in Europe in 1939, the U.S. Army began planning for the long-range defense of the Western Hemisphere against possible Axis incursion. In 1940, the then Army Air Corps (becoming the U.S. Army Air Forces after June 1941) ordered eighty additional B-17C and B-17D aircraft with more armor and armament, and by the time that the United States entered the war in 1941, Boeing was delivering the B-17E, the first variant with the distinctive tail turret.

The Flying Fortress became the nucleus of the USAAF Eighth Air Force, which would undertake the great strategic offensive against Germany. The B-17F variant, with greater range and payload capacity, was introduced in 1942, followed in 1943 by the B-17G (Model 299P), the definitive Flying Fortress. It had the ball turret, the R1820-97 engines, and all of the other B-17F improvements, as well as a forward-firing Bendix "chin" turret that made it a true Flying Fortress. It also typically carried a bomb load of nearly 10,000 pounds.

As the backbone of the great Eighth Air Force and Fifteenth Air Force air offensive against German-occupied Europe, B-17s dropped over 640,000 tons of bombs, roughly half of the overall total dropped by American bombers of all types.

Meanwhile, Boeing had begun to produce a new heavy bomber with a longer range and a greater capacity than any of the others. It went on to become the ultimate expression of strategic air power in World War II. This aircraft, which was so secret that its name could only be whispered until the war was nearly half over, was the Boeing B-29 Superfortress. It was also the aircraft that established the primacy of the Boeing Aircraft Company as the world leader in strategic bombers, positioning the company for the postwar steps that led it on the road that culminated with the B-52 Stratofortress.

The USAAF concentrated the entire force of B-29s against Japan and assigned them to the new, all-Superfortress Twentieth Air Force. The first B-29 mission was flown on June 5, 1944, and through the winter of 1944–1945, the number of B-29s grew rapidly, as did the intensity of the attacks on Japan. In March 1945, Gen. Curtis LeMay, the field commander of the Twentieth Air Force, began three-hundred-plane raids on major Japanese industrial centers, a pattern that continued through the spring and into the summer. The number of aircraft available for the missions grew, and on August 1 a total of 784 B-29s reached their targets. LeMay's plan was to defeat the Japanese from the air so that a costly ground invasion would not be necessary.

Meanwhile, the United States had developed nuclear weapons. President Harry Truman had decided to use them to force the Japanese into an unconditional surrender. Because the B-29 was the largest bomber in the USAAF, the two available atomic bombs were designed to be dropped by B-29s. Nuclear strikes would be made against Hiroshima and Nagasaki on August 6 and August 9.

By the time that the Japanese agreed to an unconditional surrender on August 15, Boeing had cinched its position as "the World Center of 4-Engine Airplane Development." The number of Flying Fortresses had reached 12,731, and nearly 3,000 Superfortresses had been produced. The planemaker on East Marginal Way was ready to move into jet bombers.

■ Left: The Boeing B-29 Superfortress was the ultimate expression of strategic air power during World War II.
■ Right: First flown in June 1947, the Boeing B-50 was a "Super" Superfortress, a variation on the World War II B-29 that featured more powerful Pratt & Whitney R4360 radial engines and a taller tail. Seen here is the B-50B variant. *USAF*

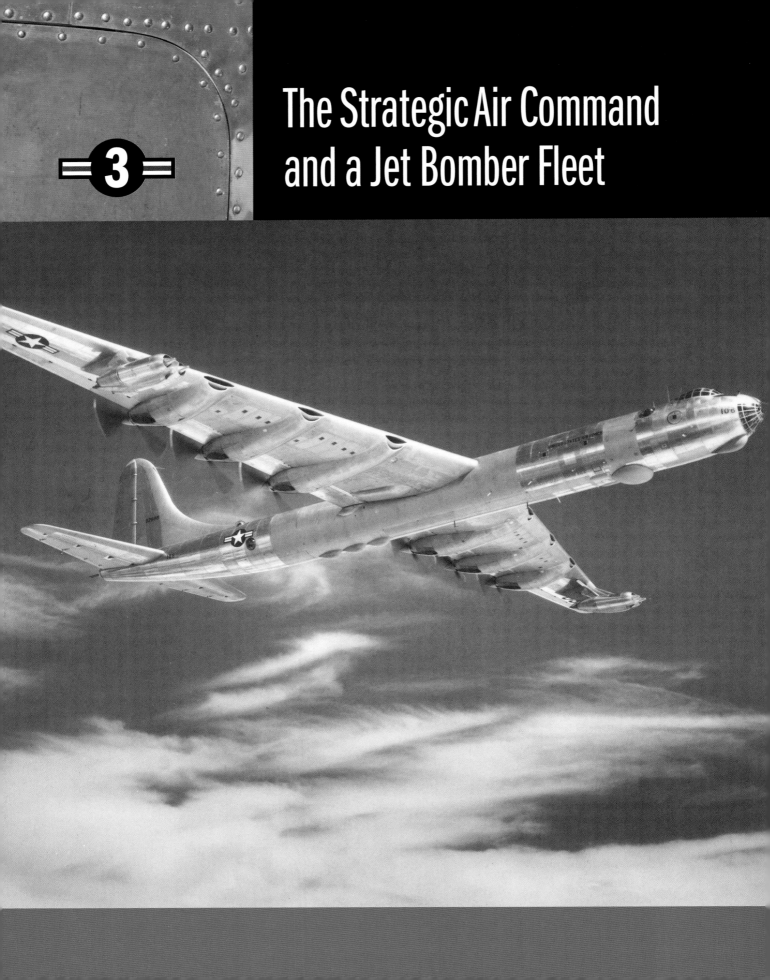

The Strategic Air Command and a Jet Bomber Fleet

3

D URING WORLD WAR II, the USAAF became the largest air force in history and, in the process, proved the importance of the strategic air power doctrine in affecting the outcome of a major war. No longer theoretical, the strategic air power doctrine was now central to the entire concept of military organization and planning. This fact would greatly influence the structure of the postwar U.S. Air Force into which the USAAF evolved in 1947.

Meanwhile, the service was reorganized, based on a view of the role of modern air power that was tempered by the experience of World War II. Combat assets were divided into separate components: the Tactical Air Command (TAC), the Air Defense Command (ADC), and, of course, the Strategic Air Command (SAC).

Gen. Carl Spaatz, the wartime commander of U.S. Strategic Air Forces in Europe, and now commanding general of the USAAF, outlined SAC's mission, stating that it would "be prepared to conduct long-range offensive operations in any part of the world either independently or in cooperation with land and naval forces; to conduct maximum-range reconnaissance over land or sea either independently or in cooperation with land and naval forces; to provide combat units capable of intense and sustained combat operations employing the latest and most advanced weapons."

In 1946, such a description was dry and theoretical against the backdrop of the euphoria brought by the end of World War II. Peace had been achieved, and all seemed well. However, even before World War II concluded, dark clouds were gathering in the east that would soon impose a new kind of war upon the world, one in which the Strategic Air Command would play a key role. This new war would be called the Cold War because it was not war in the sense of World War II, but rather an epoch of global tensions in which the world lived under the threat of World War III.

During World War II, as the Soviet Army pushed the Germans out of Eastern Europe, they used the force of arms to impose puppet governments throughout the region. While the Anglo-American Allies demobilized, the Soviet Army remained as an imposing force to dominate Eastern Europe and constituted an implicit threat to Western Europe and the rest of the world beyond. As World War II ended, a dividing line formed across Europe that Winston Churchill, Britain's wartime prime minister, referred to as the Iron Curtain.

As postwar demobilization had greatly reduced the size of the Anglo-American armies, the one ace in the hole that the United States still held was its monopoly on nuclear weapons. Therefore, the threat of nuclear weapons was the only thing that caused Stalin

■ The insignia of the Strategic Air Command was designed in 1951 by Sgt. R. T. Barnes, then assigned to the 92nd Bombardment Wing at Fairchild AFB. He was the winner of a design competition that was judged by Gen. Curtis LeMay, among others, and was awarded a $100 United States Savings Bond. *USAF*

■ Opposite:
The RB-36D reconnaissance variant preceded the B-36D bomber by two months. When it was released on September 27, 1950, this striking photo of the Convair RB-36D was described as "the first flight view released of the Air Force's intercontinental fact-finding weapon."

Left: A Boeing B-47 Stratojet carrying a Bell B-63 (later GAM-63) strategic stand-off missile. *USAF*

Right: A B-36 on the ramp at Carswell AFB, with the fuel trucks required to service the huge bomber. *USAF*

to think twice about sending his armies west of the Iron Curtain. In the early years of the Cold War, in the late 1940s, the only entity in the world that was capable of delivering nuclear weapons against a foe such as the Soviet Union was the Strategic Air Command.

For its long-range mission, SAC was initially dependant on piston-engine aircraft. SAC's early fleet was comprised of wartime B-29s, as well as Boeing B-50s, much-improved and updated variations on the B-29. Also in development in the mid-1940s was the Convair B-36 Peacemaker, an enormous bomber with an intercontinental range. It was a slow, piston-engined aircraft, but it gave SAC a range capability of 10,000 miles that would not be matched or exceeded by a jet bomber until the advent of the B-52.

The U.S. Air Force ordered its first generation of long-range jet bombers in 1947, the same year it was created. Among these was the Boeing B-47. Boeing engineers had been studying the idea of a jet bomber since 1943, and their early designs, such as the Model 424, had straight wings. When the war ended, however, Boeing's chief aerodynamicist, George Schairer, traveled to Germany with Dr. Theodore von Karman of Caltech and the group of American scientists who constituted the U.S. Army Scientific Advisory Group. Germany had led the world in jet aircraft development during the war, and the group wanted to evaluate their scientific and technical data. It was here that Schairer discovered that the 18.5-degree sweep of the Messerschmitt Me 262 wing improved performance to a significant extent.

This revelation led to Boeing recalculating and redesigning its jet bomber project. Schairer sold his boss, Ed Wells, on the idea of the swept wings, and Wells sold the concept to the USAAF. The result was the Model 448, which emerged in September 1945. Over the coming year the design was further refined, emerging finally as the six-engine Model 450 Stratojet—a futuristic airplane larger than the B-29. The USAAF ordered a pair of Stratojets under the designation XB-47. Ultimately, it would be produced in far larger numbers—more than two thousand—than any other American strategic jet bomber.

After a first flight on December 17, 1947, the Stratojet entered a flight test program that would result in a modest contract for ten B-47A production aircraft being issued ten months later. Though the prototypes were built at Plant 2 in Seattle, the production aircraft would all be built at their big Wichita facility, which had been expanded for wartime production of the B-29. While SAC's B-36 arsenal reached its peak in 1954 with

A good side view of a B-47E. Note the distinctive "starry blue" SAC stripe on the forward fuselage. *USAF*

342 of the huge planes (133 were RB-36 variants), there were more than 1,500 B-47s and RB-47s in service by 1956.

Simultaneously with the development of the warplanes, SAC was also developing the operational principles that would guide the application of strategic air power in the event that the Cold War devolved into a global nuclear war. The man who would oversee the development of the organization and tactics to make this possible was Gen. Curtis LeMay, who had presided over the defeat of Japan as commander of the B-29 force and who became SAC's commander-in-chief in October 1948. LeMay came aboard with a mandate to make SAC a force that was second to none, but found it critically lacking, not just in aircraft, but in readiness. Demobilization had created widespread demoralization. Reenlistments were down, and that was cutting the heart out of SAC's cadre of veteran pilots. Over the course of the first year and a half of his command, LeMay turned SAC into a first-rate, professional service.

It was not a moment too soon. At the beginning of the Cold War, the United States could bank on its ace-in-the-hole monopoly on nuclear weapons to make the Soviet Union think twice about launching a major armed conflict. After the Soviet detonation of its first nuclear device in 1949, the real threat of a "nuclear Pearl Harbor" became a guiding force in the formulation of American strategic policy. The Soviet sneak attack, it was theorized, could be prevented if the Russians knew their attack would result in a counterattack of greater magnitude.

In the early 1950s, the combined inventory of B-36 and B-47 bombers provided SAC with unprecedented range, bomb capacity, and speed. They were Curtis LeMay's "Big Stick." However, they were products of a passing era in the rapidly advancing world of aviation technology. The B-36 was slow, and the B-47 did not have the range needed for SAC's intercontinental mission. LeMay may have had a Big Stick, but he needed one that was both bigger and better. In Seattle, there were men at Boeing who were ready to oblige.

═ **4** ═ What We've Been Waiting For

BECAUSE TECHNOLOGY had advanced at a breathtaking pace during World War II, the immediate postwar period was an exciting time to be involved in aircraft engineering. However, in 1946, engineering was the *only* exciting place to be within the American aircraft industry.

In the space of six years, according to the *Civil Aeronautics Administration Statistical Handbook*, the American aircraft industry had built 324,750 aircraft. Of these, Boeing alone had turned out 18,229. In 1944, you could walk onto the factory floor at Plant 2 of Boeing Field in Seattle and gaze upon gleaming aluminum B-17s as far as the eye could see. In 1945, you could drive a few miles to Renton and the same was true of B-29s. In 1946, you could visit either place and practically be alone with the echo of your own voice.

Boeing's last B-17 had rolled out early in 1945, and the B-29 program wound down a year later. An order for five-thousand B-29C aircraft, scheduled for Plant 2, had been cancelled when the war ended. The B-29D program, which was redesignated as B-50A, would proceed, but only fifty-nine were ordered through all of 1946. Boeing had the Model 377 Stratocruiser airliner program in progress, but again, the numbers were small. The aircraft industry was a bad place to be unless you were an engineer lucky enough to be assigned to looking into the future.

For Boeing engineers, the future as viewed from 1946 included a number of aircraft that would never be built—jet fighters and long-range military transports—as well as a number of jet bomber concepts, such as Models 424, 432, and 448, which would eventually be funneled toward the Model 450, which in turn became the B-47.

Meanwhile, the USAAF had been sifting through the technical data compiled from the success of the B-29 deployment in the strategic air war against Japan and decided upon where it wanted to go with its next-generation strategic bomber. On the Friday after Thanksgiving 1945, the USAAF completed its overview and signed off on its conclusion. Though the first flight of the B-36 was still nine months away, they were looking to the future beyond.

The twinkle in the eye of the USAAF that became the B-52 was first seen less than a year after the end of World War II. Like the Project A and D programs a dozen years (and a technological lifetime) earlier, it was born as a design study aimed at answering a government request for proposals for an aircraft that would push the limits of performance, especially with regard to range and payload.

The official request for proposals was sent on February 13, 1946, to Martin, as well as to Convair, the builder of the B-36, and to Boeing, who had originated the B-29. The requirements in the USAAF request called for an aircraft with a cruising speed of 300 miles per hour, a service ceiling of 34,000 feet, a 5,000-mile combat radius, and a 10,000-pound bomb load.

On March 7, with Ed Wells leading the way, Boeing's engineers began work on the project, which they designated as Model 462. However, to meet the requirements in the new USAAF request, jet engines could not be specified for the long-range Model 452 because they could not supply the needed range with the state of the art in 1946.

The Model 462 took shape as straight-winged aircraft with a span of 221 feet, a shade less than that of the B-36's 230 feet. The shapes of the tail and wing design clearly showed that the 462 had roots growing out of the B-29 program. The 462 was to be powered by six Wright XT35 turboprop engines, each delivering 8,900 shaft horsepower. Boeing engineers struggled to meet the range requirement and went back to the drawing board. The result this time was the first of a long series of designs that would be designated by the company as Model 464.

The model number was first used on May 28, 1946, with the project assigned to Donald W. Finlay, who joined Boeing in 1935 and, according to company records, was "associated in project design or in preliminary design work on every multi-engine aircraft type."

The early designs, such as Models 464-16 and 464-17, retained the straight wing of the Model 462, but had a shorter wingspan and four turboprops. The scale-down was reportedly to address Air Force concerns about the cost of such a new aircraft, although when it was presented the customer expressed some reticence because the early 464 designs were not a sufficient improvement over the existing B-36.

■ It was here at the Van Cleve Hotel in downtown Dayton, Ohio, that the B-52 was born. Boeing's aerodynamic genius George Schairer went out to a hobby shop for balsa wood and glue, then sat down for a marathon weekend design session in October 1948 with Vaughn Blumenthal, Art Carlsen, Maynard Pennell, H. W. "Bob" Withington, and Ed Wells.

In the meantime, Boeing aerodynamicist George Schairer had convinced Ed Wells to exploit the potential of swept wings on jet aircraft performance. This innovation, which was about to famously transform the Model 450/B-47 program, would do the same for the Model 464. Over the course of the next two years, the Model 464 program gradually changed and evolved. By the time that the series of studies progressed to the Models 464-29 through 464-35 series, the proposed aircraft's wings had a span of 185 feet and a 20-degree sweep, but the plane was still intended to be powered by four XT35 turboprops.

At the same time that the Model 464 strategic bomber was working its way across the Boeing drafting tables, one of the other projects taking shape at Boeing was a smaller, shorter-range turboprop medium bomber similar in size and shape to the Model 450/B-47. When the B-47 made its first flight in December 1947 with six jet engines, its initial success and promise led to Boeing winning a contract in June 1948 to build a successor bomber under the designation B-55. This aircraft, the Boeing Model 479, would be like the Model 474, but powered by six jet engines.

The larger Model 464, meanwhile, was still designed to fly with turboprops driving contra-rotating propellers. Such was the configuration that was to be submitted to the U.S. Air Force in October 1948, specifically to the Air Materiel Command (AMC) at Wright-Patterson AFB, better known as Wright-Pat, near Dayton, Ohio. The AMC and its predecessors had been the technical gateway by which new aircraft passed muster since before the U.S. Air Force was the Army Air Corps, and the base long known as Wright Field was established literally across the road from where the Wright brothers tested their earliest airplanes.

Two of the men most responsible for the B-52 were Boeing chief aerodynamicist George S. Schairer (left) and Boeing chief engineer Edward Curtis Wells.

George Schairer, accompanied by fellow aerodynamicist Vaughn Blumenthal and Art Carlsen from the production department, hand-carried the "final" Model 464-49 proposal to Wright-Patterson. The wing was still swept at 20 degrees, and the aircraft was still powered by four turboprops driving contra-rotating propellers—but the turboprop of choice had changed because of concerns about the durability of the shaft of the XT35 at high rpm. Pratt & Whitney, the largest American producer of piston engines during World War II, had started developing turboprop engines, and their TP4 (T45) engine was selected for the Model 464 program in 1947.

The presentation was scheduled for the morning of Thursday, October 21. Coincidentally, this was exactly two days after Curtis LeMay assumed command of SAC. Of course, LeMay was not present at Wright-Pat that day, but Gen. Kenneth Bonner "K. B." Wolfe was. The man who had commanded the first operational B-29s during World War II, Wolfe had long been involved in the development and procurement of bombers, and he was now in charge of bomber acquisition for the AMC.

Sitting next to Wolfe across the table that morning was Col. Henry "Pete" Warden. An MIT-trained engineer, Warden had flown as a fighter pilot in the Philippines

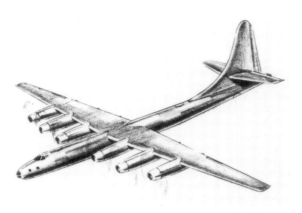

■ The Model 462 was Boeing's first postwar heavy bomber to be more than a Model 345 (B-29/B-50) derivative aircraft.

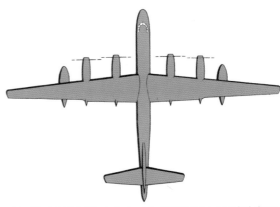

■ The Model 464-17 started out in 1946 to be a scaled-down, four-engine 462, but it was scaled up to a span of 205 feet and a gross weight of 400,000 pounds.

■ The Model 464-29 emerged in August 1947 with increased wing area and a 20-degree sweep to the leading edge.

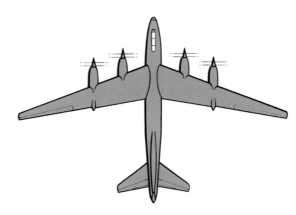

■ The Model 464-35 of early 1948 looked a bit like a turboprop Model 450 (B-47), but with a 20-degree sweep to the whole wing. This was the proposal that George Schairer, Ed Wells, and the others presented in October 1948.

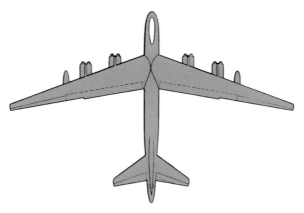

■ The Model 464-40 was the result of an Air Force request in May 1948 to take a look at a jet-propelled variant of the Model 464-35.

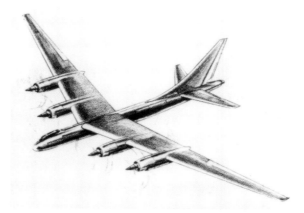

■ The Model 464-41 of 1948 had the same swept tail as the Models 464-35 and 464-40, but longer wings.

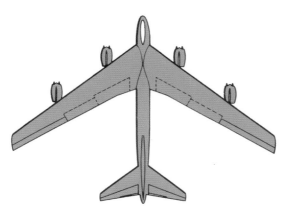

■ The Model 464-49 was the result of the famous redesign session in the Van Cleve Hotel. It had the jet engines that the Air Force demanded, eight of them, and the wing sweep was increased to 35 degrees.

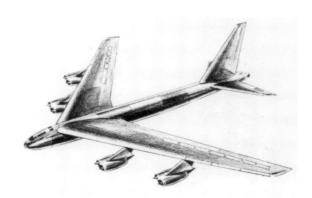

■ The Model 464-54 was like the Model 464-49 in most respects, but the gracefully swept tail seen in the Models 464-35, 464-40, and 464-49 was replaced with the sharply angled, business-like tail that would be used on the B-52.

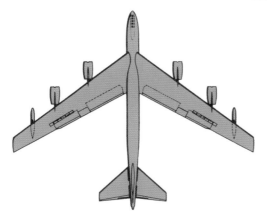

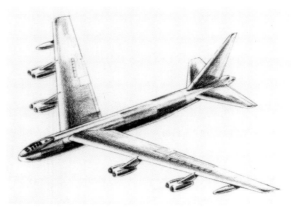

■ The Model 464-67 had an extended forward fuselage and a Model 464-54 tail, but was otherwise much like the Model 464-49 that rode down in the Van Cleve elevator with the Boeing "Dream Team" in October 1948. It was built as a flyable aircraft under the designations XB-52 and YB-52.

The dramatic rollout on the rainy night in November 1951. The mysteriously shrouded machine was the harbinger of a new chapter in Boeing and USAF history. No one could have imagined that night how long the chapter would last.

in the early days of World War II and had been at Wright Field since 1944. Having been involved in acquisition of both the B-36 and B-47, Warden had studied jet bombers to nearly the same extent as the Boeing men had. In so doing, he had developed some strong opinions.

The meeting was over almost as quickly as it began. Warden took one look at Schairer's drawing and told him that if he did not "get rid of those propellers," he would recommend that Boeing's proposal be rejected. The state of the art had changed considerably since 1946, and the Air Force now insisted on *jet* bombers. This came as a bit of a surprise to the Boeing men, given that they had previously suggested jet propulsion in their 464-40 concept and had been rejected.

Schairer asked the AMC men for another meeting to present a revised proposal. Warden agreed to schedule them for the following Monday, October 25—*if* they could meet the specifications and get rid of the propellers.

Schairer phoned Ed Wells, who was on the next plane out of Seattle. He then went to a hobby shop and bought an armload of balsa wood and some glue. In the meantime, two other Boeing engineers, Maynard Pennell and H. W. "Bob" Withington, happened to be in town to work on the B-55 program. By Thursday night, this six-man "dream team" of Boeing technical expertise were together at the Van Cleve Hotel in downtown Dayton for a marathon redesign session. Wells sketched the new airplane freehand, while the

The YB-52 on the ramp at Boeing Field, with test markings on its fuselage and tires. The first flight of the YB-52, the first Stratofortress to fly, came on April 15, 1952, with Tex Johnston at the controls.

others calculated and recalculated performance parameters. This weekend has long been a cornerstone of Boeing corporate lore. The result was a jet bomber that they called the Model 464-49.

On Monday morning (though some sources say it was Wednesday), Schairer, Wells, and the others were back at Wright-Pat with a proposal and a balsa-wood model—and *no* propellers. Instead, Boeing would use eight of Pratt & Whitney's new J57-P-3 turbojet engines, paired in pods beneath the wings of each bomber. Having been developing the turboprop engines for the Model 464 program in its earlier configuration, Pratt & Whitney was eager to remain with the program.

Another change that would be very important to the future of the aircraft was an increase in wing area from less than 3,000 square feet to 4,000 square feet. Wing area is an important factor in long-range operations, and the Boeing engineers felt that a mistake had been made in giving the B-47 a smaller, 1,400-square-foot wing. As with the B-47, the wing of the new aircraft was supported with outrigger landing gear on the wingtips.

Warden liked what he saw on this go-round and promptly departed for Washington, hand-carrying both the proposal and the model, to recommend that the U.S. Air Force acquire two full-scale prototypes. On November 17, the proposal was approved by the Air Force, and a full-scale mock-up was ordered.

A close-up view of the B-47-type canopy that was common to the XB-52 and YB-52. Curtis LeMay insisted that it be abandoned for side-by-side seating in production series aircraft, and it was.

After the mock-up was inspected in April 1949, and further refinements were made to the design, General LeMay recommended in early 1950 that the Air Force acquire the aircraft, now designated as Model 464-67. Two virtually identical Model 464-67 jets were ordered under the XB-52 designation, but one would be completed as a service test YB-52 for accounting reasons, though there are varying accounts as to the specifics.

The name *Stratofortress* was coined with reference to the earlier Boeing Flying Fortress and Superfortress, with a nod to Boeing's Strato airliners, specifically the Model 307 Stratoliner and Model 377 Stratocruiser.

More than three decades later, Walter Boyne of the Smithsonian National Air and Space Museum asked Wells, Schairer, and others what they "might have done differently with the B-52 if they had had an opportunity now to change it."

Boyne reports that "each of the men thought the question over carefully, and each came to the conclusion that given the knowledge available at the time, they would not change the design in any way."

Indeed, the 464-67 aircraft were, at a glance, nearly identical to George Schairer's hand-carved model. The wing remained at 185 feet as it had been since the swept wing was adopted. Like the model, the sweep in the 464-67 was changed from 20 to 35 degrees, the same as on the B-47. One difference was that the fuselage was lengthened by 13 feet 11 inches to 152 feet 8 inches.

Ironically, a casualty of this turn of events was the B-55 program. If the Air Force already had the B-47, and if they were now soon to have a high-performance jet bomber with intercontinental range, what did they need with another jet *medium* bomber?

Meanwhile, the Air Force had also approved a competing proposal from Convair. Because of the high priority attached to a strategic jet bomber, they decided to order two prototypes from Boeing's rival as well and then evaluate the two pairs side by side. The Convair proposal, designated as the YB-60, was essentially a production B-36 fuselage with swept wings. Like the B-52 prototypes, each YB-60 would be powered by eight Pratt & Whitney J57-P-3 turbojets.

Across the globe, the Soviet Union was also working on a strategic bomber with intercontinental range. Developed by the design bureau headed by Andrei Tupolev, this aircraft was nearly as large as the B-52 and it had the same parent—insofar as Tupolev had entered the field of large strategic bombers by *reverse-engineering* copies of the Boeing B-29 Superfortress! These aircraft, which had been interned in the Soviet Union after raids on Japan during World War II, had been meticulously copied as the Tupolev Tu-4.

Tupolev's new intercontinental bomber, originally designated as the Tu-20, first flew in 1952 and had the same 35-degree wing sweep as the B-52—another feature "borrowed" from Boeing. Unlike Boeing, though, Tupolev stuck with turboprop engines driving contra-rotating propellers, exactly as Boeing had proposed in the Model 464-35. Designated as Tu-95, this aircraft would be a mainstay of Soviet strategic air power throughout the Cold War, and it was still flying in the twenty-first century.

Formal Debut

On the rainy night of November 29, 1951, East Marginal Way was closed to traffic, and a huge airplane, draped with hundreds of square yards of white muslin, was towed across the street to Boeing Field. Some say that it was concealed for security reasons because Boeing and the Air Force wanted to conceal it from prying Soviet eyes, but others have suggested wryly that it was merely for dramatic effect.

Some sources say that the airplane was the XB-52 (tail number 49-230), while others say that it was the YB-52 (tail number 49-231), because the YB-52 was the first to fly. Originally it was said that delays in equipment installation put the XB-52 behind schedule, but in later years, information has come to light to suggest that it was because the XB-52's pneumatic system malfunctioned during tests, and the wings were damaged.

With its wheels rotating into the wheel wells, the YB-52 takes off for a test flight, circa 1952.

Alvin "Tex" Johnston, the legendary Boeing test pilot, was in the pilot's seat for taxi tests, as well as for the April 15, 1952, debut flight of the YB-52. Col. Guy Townsend, the U.S. Air Force's program man, was flying as copilot.

"The historic importance of this initial flight was in my mind as I taxied into position," Johnston recalls in his memoirs. "Boeing Field's single runway stretched ahead past the company ramp, with city streets and hillsides crowded with men and women whose hopes and dreams hinged on the success of this airplane. With temperatures and pressures normal, all takeoff checks completed, and takeoff clearance, I advanced the throttles to 100-percent power and released the brakes. With an awesome eight-engine roar, the YB-52 sprang forward, accelerating rapidly, wings curving upward as they accepted the 235,000-pound initial flight gross weight. At [takeoff speed] the airplane lifted off the runway, because of the 6-degree angle of incidence of the wing, and at 11:08 a.m. we were airborne. . . . At three hours and eight minutes, the flight of the YB-52 [to Larson AFB in Moses Lake, Washington] was the longest duration maiden flight in the history of aviation and it introduced one of the world's great airplanes."

The first Convair YB-60 made its debut flight three days later. The XB-52 followed on October 2, but by then the YB-60 program had been terminated, the aircraft having proven itself to be too slow.

In demonstrating the Stratofortress for President Dwight Eisenhower, Tex Johnston took off with a partial fuel load and a light gross weight, which permitted a spectacular

The Boeing YB-52, circa 1953. *USAF*

climb-out angle and a steep left chandelle as he brought the Stratofortress back over the field at 300 feet.

After the flight, Johnston invited Eisenhower aboard for a cockpit tour, "which the president accepted, much to the alarm of the Secret Service agents." With the president seated in the pilot's seat, he explained the cockpit and the president "made it clear that he was amazed that an airplane of such magnitude could execute the flight maneuvers he had witnessed. So were many other people."

Like the B-47, both the XB-52 and YB-52 prototypes had tandem seating for the flight crew under a narrow teardrop canopy. After LeMay's first flight in the YB-52, Boeing president Bill Allen asked "How do you like her, General?"

As Tex Johnston writes, "LeMay lit a cigar, placed the Zippo lighter in his pocket, looked Allen in the eye, and said, 'You have a hell of an airplane, Allen. As soon as you put a side-by-side cockpit on it, I'll buy some.'" The Boeing team quickly redesigned the flight deck for side-by-side seating in all subsequent aircraft.

Recalling his own first flight in the B-52 with LeMay aboard, Johnston explains that he rolled to a 40-degree bank, executed a 180-degree turn, rolled to 40 degrees in the opposite direction, pulled around another 180 degrees, and said, "'It's all yours.' [LeMay] wasn't bashful. He executed several identical maneuvers and said, 'This is what we've been waiting for.'"

5 Production and Model Evolution

THE STRATOFORTRESS was formally ordered into production on December 16, 1952, less than three months after the first flight of the XB-52. The initial order called for thirteen B-52As (Model 464-201-0), but only three were built, as more of a service test series. By the time of the first flight, the other ten had been redesignated as RB-52B reconnaissance variants (Model 464-201-3) with an increased gross weight, designed to carry crewed reconnaissance pods in their bomb bays.

The pods had the capability of carrying a variety of optical equipment, including K-17, K-22, K-36, or K-38 cameras, as well as T-11 mapping cameras. Electronic equipment carried included AN/APR-9, AN/APR-14, and AN/ARR-88 panoramic radar receivers. Photoflash bombs were also carried in the bomb bay adjacent to the pod. The pods were removable, so that the aircraft could still be used to carry bombs. In fact, unlike the B-47, which was widely used in a reconnaissance role, the RB-52Bs were rarely flown with their pods.

Originally ordered in June 1952, the "B" series was to have been comprised entirely of RB-52B reconnaissance aircraft, but additional orders for RB-52Bs alternated with orders for B-52B bombers (Model 464-201-4) after 1953. In the end, twenty-seven RB-52Bs and twenty-three B-52Bs were built. Because of the infrequent use of the reconnaissance capability, the Air Force generally referred to the fleet simply by the B-52B designation. In fact, the aircraft delivered as B-52B also had the capability of accommodating the pods, so the differences were slight.

One difference which did set the B model apart from other Stratofortresses was the tail gun arrangement. While the turrets of all other variants, from the B-52A through the B-52G, used the quad-fifty arrangement of four .50-caliber machine guns, the turrets of eighteen RB-52Bs and sixteen B-52Bs were delivered with a pair of M24A1 20mm cannons and an MD-5 fire control system.

The Stratofortress production series aircraft evolved quickly. The first B-52A (Model 464-201-0) made its maiden flight on August 5, 1954, followed by the first B-52B (Model 464-201-3) on January 25, 1955. The first of thirty-five B-52Cs (Model 464-201-6) took to the air on March 9, 1956. Like all the "B" models, the B-52Cs were built with a reconnaissance capability but were designated as B-52C rather than RB-52C. The B-52C was also equipped with the AN/ASB-15 navigation and bombing system, an improvement over the Sperry K-3A bombing system of the B-52B.

Through the eleventh B-52B, the engines for the Stratofortress were Pratt & Whitney J57-P-1Ws, like those of the prototypes but with water injection for improved

A head-on view of the B-52B assembly line at Boeing Field in Seattle. Note the tipped-down position of the tail, a feature that permitted the huge bomber to be built in a factory that once built B-17s.

performance. As the aircraft rolled out, the engines were gradually upgraded to J57-P-19W standard in the B-52B and J57-P-29W in the B-52C.

Other detail differences between the two prototypes and the production aircraft included provisions for 1,000-gallon external fuel tanks and inflight refueling. Boeing had become a pioneer in the practical application of the latter in routine operations and had earlier adapted its piston-engine C-97 Stratofreighter (Model 367) to serve as the U.S. Air Force's principal aerial tanker.

By the time that the Stratofortress entered production, Boeing had developed a jet refueling aircraft, the KC-135 (Model 717) Stratotanker. The KC-135 and B-52 would enter service at the same time and would be inexorably linked with one another in SAC operations for decades.

The external fuel tanks, built by Fairchild, meanwhile, would become an issue in the early stages of Stratofortress production when they did not fit. The first reaction from Art Carlsen, the production man who was now the B-52 project chief, was to make Fairchild fix the problem. However, Thorton Arnold "T" Wilson, an MIT-trained engineer who had been with the Model 464 program since the early days, suggested that this solution would adversely impact the schedule and that Boeing itself had the expertise to fix the problem. He was right. T Wilson succeeded Bill Allen as Boeing president in 1968.

Seated side by side as required by LeMay, the pilot and copilot of the production series Stratofortresses shared the upper level of the pressurized flight deck with the Electronic Countermeasures (ECM) operator, while two bombardier-navigators were in the lower deck below them. The gunner was positioned in the tail turret.

The crew positions on the upper flight deck—pilot, copilot, and ECM officer—were equipped with ejection seats that ejected upward. Lower-deck crew positions used downward-ejecting seats that could not be safely used below 200 feet. To escape, the tail gunner would jettison the tail gun assembly and bail out through the resulting hole.

Offensive armament comprised up to 43,000 pounds of ordnance in the 28-foot bomb bay, though a smaller load was typical in order to achieve optimal range. The payload

■ Pratt & Whitney J57 turbojet engines are hung on the wings of a B-52B. Examples of this variant were delivered with a wide range of water-injected J57 models.

■ The first of the three B-52A Stratofortresses made its debut flight on August 5, 1954. The series served as a service test, rather than operational, series. USAF

■ The RB-52B was the only Stratofortress variant to be specifically designated as a reconnaissance aircraft, although in practice, the aircraft were mostly configured as bombers. USAF

■ B-52C forward fuselages take shape on the factory floor. Note the open doors into which the ejection seats will be lowered.

■ The B-52C Stratofortresses are said to have been the first that were all delivered from the factory with gloss white paint on their undersurfaces. The paint was intended to reflect the radiation of the nuclear blast from the bombs they dropped. *USAF*

■ A detail view of the manned tail turret of a B-52D. Most early model Stratofortresses were equipped with four .50-caliber machine guns in this quad-fifty arrangement.

included twenty-seven 1,000-pound conventional bombs, or a nuclear load. Initially, the Stratofortress carried an 8,500-pound Mk 6 uranium fission atomic bomb and, later, a pair of 7,600-pound Mk 15 thermonuclear bombs, also known as hydrogen bombs, or H-bombs. Thermonuclear weapons derive their destructive force from the fusion of hydrogen atoms (deuterium and tritium) and are more powerful than fission weapons.

All B-52s were delivered from the factory in natural metal finish, but, beginning with the B-52C, the Stratofortresses were delivered with their undersides painted gloss white to reflect the thermal radiation expected from the blast from the nuclear weapon that the aircraft dropped. B-52Bs seen with white bellies were painted after delivery.

On May 21, 1956, a B-52B became the first aircraft to drop a thermonuclear weapon when it released a Mk 15 at Bikini Atoll in a test code-named Cherokee, which was part of Operation Redwing. The Mk 15 was in service with SAC fleet for about a decade, beginning in 1955.

It was superseded from 1957 by several other types. They included the 15,000-pound Mk 21, which had a destructive force of up to five megatons, and the 6,750-pound Mk 39 (later W39), with a 3.8-megaton yield. The B-52s also flew with the smaller Mk 28 (later B28), which had a maximum yield, depending on variant, of 1.45 megatons. In the 1960s, more advanced thermonuclear weapons such as the 9-megaton B53 and the variable-yield B61 became available for the B-52 arsenal and earlier types were phased out.

Beginning with the B-52D series (Model 464-201-7), Boeing opened a second source of Stratofortress production. Back in 1946, when Boeing was first thinking about the airplane that became the Stratofortress, the factory complex at Seattle and Renton was a ghost town. By the time that the B-52C was on the assembly line, this "town" was becoming very crowded. Boeing was beginning production of the KC-135, as well its revolutionary Model 707 jetliner. Meanwhile, however, Boeing's other center of production was winding down. The facility in Wichita, Kansas, which Boeing had acquired when it bought Stearman Aircraft in 1934, had been a major center of B-29 production during World War II, and Boeing had built all the production B-47s there. With B-47 production ending, and a large workforce in place, Boeing began shifting Stratofortress manufacturing to Wichita.

Seattle would build 101 B-52Ds, while Wichita produced 69. There were 42 B-52Es (Model 464-259) and 44 B-52Fs (Model 464-260) built in Seattle, while Wichita produced 58 and 45, respectively. Externally, the early-production series Stratofortresses, from B-52B through B-52F were virtually indistinguishable. Internally, upgrades to electronic equipment that were introduced in new models were often retrofitted in some examples of earlier models.

The first flight of a B-52D was at Wichita on May 14, 1956, more than four months ahead of the first Seattle B-52D. The B-52E first flew on October 3, 1957, and the B-52F made its debut on May 6, 1958. The former used the same J57-P-19W and J57-P-29W engines as its predecessors, while the latter was powered by J57-P-43W engines.

An important innovation first seen in the B-52E was the advanced, automated IBM AN/ASQ-38 bombing-navigation system, which permitted low-level operations. This included an improved search radar receiver-transmitter and newly developed terrain avoidance compute with terrain avoidance displays and controls for the pilot and copilot. Though it caused problems initially, when the bugs were worked out the AN/ASQ-38 was a significant improvement over the mechanical analog Sperry K-System, dating from the late 1940s, that was used in earlier model Stratofortresses.

The New Generation

As the initial six B-52 models were in production and appearing in rapid succession—with an average of just nine months between model introductions—Boeing engineers were thinking ahead toward the Model 464-253, a substantially improved second generation of Stratofortresses.

The presentation to the Air Force of this new generation aircraft took place in March 1956 and included a number of proposed technical upgrades aimed at improving performance and reducing airframe weight. Among other things, the Boeing proposal promised a 30 percent increase in unrefueled range, along with a 25 percent decrease in maintenance man-hours.

After months of consideration and back-and-forth, the U.S. Air Force approved Boeing's proposal with a letter contract dated August 29, 1957. A big part of the Air Force decision is said to have been the problems and delays in the development of the Convair B-58 Hustler supersonic strategic bomber.

A series of three orders, issued through April 28, 1959, called for a total of 193 Boeing Model 464-253 aircraft to be delivered under the designation B-52G. This was by far the largest number of Stratofortresses of any model. With B-52 production now terminated in Seattle, all of the B-52Gs would be built at Wichita.

Though the B-52G was designed for the same J57-P-43W engines introduced on the B-52F, the aircraft was substantially different in many other ways.

The most outwardly apparent change was in the size of the tail, which, at 40 feet 8 inches, was a full 8 feet shorter than those of the "tall-tailed" first generation of B-52s. However, this was only the tip of the proverbial iceberg. Combined with the elimination of the aileron system in a newly redesigned wing, this reduced the overall empty weight by an amazing 6 tons. Another 3 tons was saved in the wing redesign by making it a "wet wing" through the inclusion of integral fuel tanks.

Conversely, the *gross* weight increased by 19 tons, as the weight savings were more than offset by the increased fuel capacity of nearly 7,000 gallons. This increased the range capability of the B-52G by better than 30 percent.

Other revisions in the new design concerned provisions for the crew, notably the relocation of the tail gunner from his lonely outpost in the tail to a seat adjacent to the ECM operator in the forward fuselage. Here, he operated the new Avco-Crosley AN/ASG-15 fire control system by remote control.

The most welcome change, so far as the other crewmembers were concerned, was a revision of the climate control system. A long-standing complaint was that while the pilot and copilot roasted in the sun, the crewmembers below shivered in the cold. The B-52G afforded separate climate control options.

A Block 60 Seattle-built B-52D is seen over snowcapped western mountains as it might have appeared over snowcapped Siberian mountains had the Cold War turned hot.

■ The first Seattle-built B-52E during low-level flight testing off the coast of the Pacific Northwest, circa 1957. The B-52E and B-52F were both factory-equipped with radar that permitted low-altitude operations. *USAF*

■ A Block 75 Wichita-built B-52G is refueled by a KC-135A high over a snow-covered Midwestern landscape. The first B-52G entered service in February 1959. *USAF*

The IBM AN/ASQ-38 bombing-navigation system introduced on the B-52F was also retained in the B-52G as built, but this would be subject to numerous electronics upgrades through the coming decades.

The B-52G made its first flight on August 31, 1958, and the type entered service with the Strategic Air Command's 5th Bombardment Wing at Travis AFB on February 13, 1959.

By then, Boeing was already working on the aircraft that would be the "ultimate Stratofortress," the Model 464-261. The final B-52 type, it was first ordered on May 6, 1960, under the designation B-52H. A subsequent order, issued six weeks later, brought the total number of B-52Hs to 102, all of which were built at Wichita. This also brought the total number of Stratofortresses of all types to 744.

Structurally, the B-52H was like the B-52G, with the wet wing and shorter tail. What made it such a significant improvement, and what set it apart visually, were the engines. The water-injected J57 turbojets were now superseded by eight Pratt & Whitney TF33-P-3 turbofans. This engine was based on the commercial JT3D turbofan, which was then becoming the turbojet replacement of choice for many airlines.

The greater thrust of the turbofan engine type provides improved takeoff performance at higher gross weights, while being significantly quieter and more fuel efficient. Of particular interest to SAC was a 20 percent increase in range over that of the B-52G.

The broader engine nacelles of the TF33s were a notable difference in appearance between the B-52G and B-52H, as was the revised tail armament. The quad-fifty

An inflight photo of the fourth B-52G, to be built at Wichita, a Block 75 bird.

A photographer arrives at Boeing Field in Seattle in his Austin Healey to watch the rollout of a Block 110 B-52F. The first of the F models made its debut in May 1958.

arrangement and AN/ASG-15 fire control system were superseded by a six-barreled General Electric M61 rotary cannon with 1,242 rounds of 20mm ammunition and an Emerson AN/ASG-21 fire control system.

Digital electronics to allow routine low-level operations, which had been introduced in the B-52E and B-52F, continued to be a key part of the factory equipment on the B-52G and B-52H, and it would be subject to further in-service upgrades through the years on both aircraft.

The B-52H made its first flight on July 20, 1960, although the TF33 turbofan engines had previously been tested on a B-52G, making this aircraft a "virtual B-52H."

The first delivery of a B-52H to SAC went to the 379th Bombardment Wing at Wurtsmith AFB in Michigan on May 9, 1961, and the last of the 102 B-52H aircraft was received by the 4136th Strategic Wing at Minot AFB on October 26, 1962.

In the meantime, wing cracks were identified on a small number of B-52H aircraft. These were traced to fasteners at the wing roots that were prone to corrosion, and the issue was corrected.

No Friend of Manned Bombers

On the same day that SAC received its last B-52H, the last Convair B-58 was delivered to the 305th Bombardment Wing at Bunker Hill AFB in Indiana. This brought production of both aircraft to an end. As the official SAC history reports, "for the first time since 1946 there was no bomber being produced or developed for SAC. The XB-70 was the only bomber-type aircraft under development and it had been excluded from consideration as a bomber. In September, an Air Force recommendation to expand the XB-70 program into a full-scale weapon system development was rejected by the Department of Defense."

The narrative goes on to say that four days after the final deliveries, "Secretary of Defense [Robert] McNamara requested the Air Force 'consider an alternative bombing system' as a follow-on [from] the B-52, something that could serve as an airborne missile launching platform for the period beyond 1970."

Robert Strange McNamara came to Washington in 1961 as defense secretary under President John F. Kennedy and remained in that post under Lyndon B. Johnson until 1968. In this role, he was historically instrumental in guiding the shape of weapons acquisition—and in guiding American involvement in the Vietnam War.

He was greatly fascinated by strategic missiles and had little enthusiasm for strategic bombers. A strong proponent of ICBMs over manned bombers in a nuclear deterrent force, he fast-tracked the Minuteman solid-fuel ICBM, while ordering the termination of XB-70 development, as well as other manned programs—such as the Boeing X-20, which would have been America's first space shuttle.

Nevertheless, the Air Force did undertake a number of manned bomber feasibility studies during his tenure. These included the Low-Altitude Manned Penetrator (LAMP) and the Advanced Manned Precision Strike System (AMPSS) projects in 1963, which culminated in the Advanced Manned Strategic Aircraft (AMSA) program of 1964.

Stratofortress Production by Model Number

(See Appendix 2 for more detail)

XB-52 (Boeing Model 464-67)
1 built in Seattle

YB-52 (Boeing Model 464-67)
1 built in Seattle

B-52A (Boeing Model 464-201-0)
3 built in Seattle

B-52B (Boeing Model 464-201-4)
23 built in Seattle in 3 blocks

RB-52B (Boeing Model 464-201-3)
27 built in Seattle in 6 blocks

B-52C (Boeing Model 464-201-6)
35 built in Seattle in 3 blocks

B-52D (Boeing Model 464-201-7)
101 built in Seattle in 6 blocks
69 built in Wichita in 10 blocks

B-52E 59 (Boeing Model 464-259)
42 built in Seattle in 4 blocks
58 built in Wichita in 4 blocks

B-52F (Boeing Model 464-260)
44 built in Seattle in 3 blocks
45 built in Wichita in 2 blocks

B-52G (Boeing Model 464-253)
193 built in Wichita in 12 blocks

B-52H (Boeing Model 464-261)
102 built in Wichita in 9 blocks

Total: 774

Production Close-Up
Boeing B-52 Stratofortress

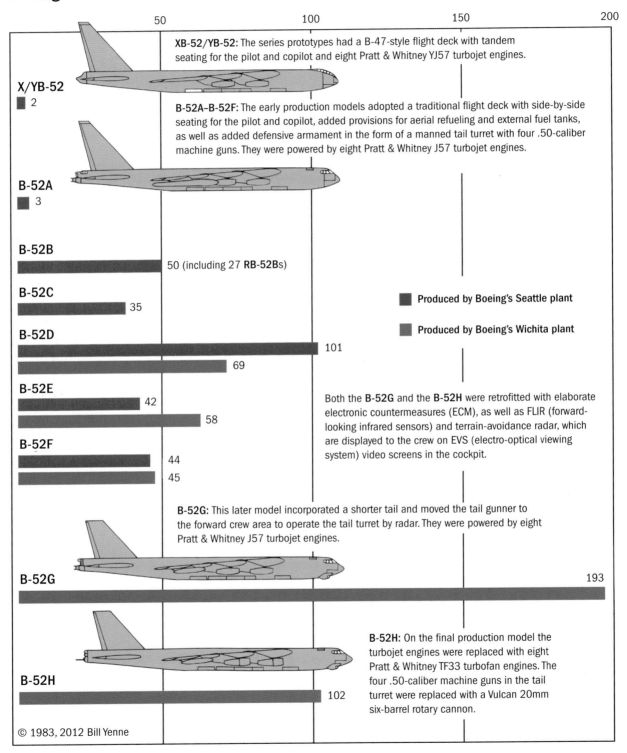

50   100   150   200

XB-52/YB-52: The series prototypes had a B-47-style flight deck with tandem seating for the pilot and copilot and eight Pratt & Whitney YJ57 turbojet engines.

X/YB-52
■ 2

B-52A–B-52F: The early production models adopted a traditional flight deck with side-by-side seating for the pilot and copilot, added provisions for aerial refueling and external fuel tanks, as well as added defensive armament in the form of a manned tail turret with four .50-caliber machine guns. They were powered by eight Pratt & Whitney J57 turbojet engines.

B-52A
■ 3

B-52B
50 (including 27 **RB-52B**s)

■ **Produced by Boeing's Seattle plant**

■ **Produced by Boeing's Wichita plant**

B-52C
35

B-52D
101
69

Both the **B-52G** and the **B-52H** were retrofitted with elaborate electronic countermeasures (ECM), as well as FLIR (forward-looking infrared sensors) and terrain-avoidance radar, which are displayed to the crew on EVS (electro-optical viewing system) video screens in the cockpit.

B-52E
42
58

B-52F
44
45

B-52G: This later model incorporated a shorter tail and moved the tail gunner to the forward crew area to operate the tail turret by radar. They were powered by eight Pratt & Whitney J57 turbojet engines.

B-52G
193

B-52H: On the final production model the turbojet engines were replaced with eight Pratt & Whitney TF33 turbofan engines. The four .50-caliber machine guns in the tail turret were replaced with a Vulcan 20mm six-barrel rotary cannon.

B-52H
102

© 1983, 2012 Bill Yenne

Ironically, the man most responsible for AMSA was Harold Brown, who had been chief of research and engineering at the Pentagon since 1961 and who had been instrumental in killing the XB-70 program. In 1965, Lyndon Johnson named him as Secretary of the Air Force, directly under McNamara.

The winning AMSA proposal, submitted by North American Rockwell, appeared after McNamara and Brown had left office and was ordered into production by the Nixon administration under the designation B-1A. This aircraft made its first flight on December 23, 1974, but the program was terminated by the Carter administration after only four were built.

The Air Force resumed studies of a new strategic bomber in 1979 under the Long-Range Combat Aircraft (LRCA) project. A Rockwell proposal based on the B-1A was approved by the Reagan administration in October 1981, and the first of 100 B-1Bs made its debut on March 23, 1983. The B-1B reached its initial operational capability on October 1, 1986, twenty-four years after the last delivery of a B-52H.

■ The second of 102 Wichita-built B-52Hs. The H Model was visually distinguishable by its low tail, its turbofan engines, and the Vulcan cannon in its tail turret.

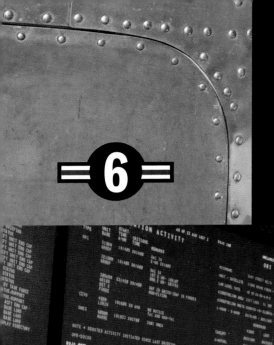

O N JUNE 29, 1955, SAC's first B-52B was flown from Seattle to Castle AFB, piloted by Brig. Gen. William E. Eubank, commander of the 93rd Bombardment Wing. Located near Merced in California's San Joaquin Valley, Castle would remain as a center of B-52 crew training base for several decades.

In June 1956, the 42nd Bombardment Wing at Loring AFB in Maine became the second wing to be equipped with B-52s, and the first B-36 unit to convert to the Stratofortress. The 99th Bombardment Wing at Westover AFB, Massachusetts, became the third B-52 wing in December 1956. From here, the incorporation of the Stratofortress into the U.S. Air Force proceeded quickly. The 92nd Bombardment Wing at Fairchild AFB in Washington and the 28th at Ellsworth AFB, South Dakota, came next, in 1957.

From 18 B-52s in the Strategic Air Command fleet at the end of 1955, the inventory grew to 97 at the end of 1956 and to 243 in December of 1957, the last year that Curtis LeMay was in charge of SAC. When LeMay moved up the ladder to assume the post of Air Force Vice Chief of Staff, he handed SAC off to his handpicked successor, Gen. Thomas S. Power, who would remain in that post until 1964.

During his last year at SAC's helm, and eager to demonstrate the potential of his new bomber—both to the Soviet Union and to the budget-conscious United States Congress—LeMay ordered a succession of dramatic demonstration flights.

First, around the continent. On November 24–25, 1956, in Operation Quick Kick, eight B-52s made highly publicized nonstop flights around the northern perimeter of North America, flying as far north as the North Pole to demonstrate the capability of SAC to reach the Soviet Union across the top of the world. Four Stratofortress from the 93rd Bombardment Wing arced eastward from Castle, while four from the 42nd arced westward from Loring.

The official SAC history notes that "the flight demonstrated both the value and the limitations of the KC-97 tanker. Without the four inflight refuelings, the flight would have been impossible; but with a higher, faster-flying [KC-135] jet tanker, refuelings could have been conducted much faster. According to Colonel [Marcus L.] Hill's estimation, his flying time could have been reduced by at least three hours by using the KC-135."

SAC began receiving its first KC-135s at Castle AFB in June 1957. Thereafter, the team effort formed by the B-52s and the KC-135 would remain the cornerstone of SAC air power through the end of the Cold War.

Next, around the entire globe. In 1957, LeMay initiated Operation Power Flite, intended to circumnavigate the earth with three B-52Bs. Eight years earlier, he had

The SAC war room deep inside the bomb-proof bowels of Offutt AFB. *USAF*

sent a Boeing B-50 Superfortress from the 43rd Bombardment Group to fly around the world nonstop. The first aircraft to do so, it accomplished the feat in ninety-four hours by using inflight refueling.

On January 16, 1957, five Stratofortresses—three primaries and two spares—took off from Castle AFB led by Maj. Gen. Archie Old, commander of SAC's Fifteenth Air Force. The three primary aircraft went on to be refueled in-flight over the North Atlantic, North Africa, the Indian Ocean, and the Pacific by KC-97 aerial tankers.

The flight plan called for the lead aircraft to land at the Fifteenth Air Force headquarters at March AFB in Southern California, with the other two returning to Castle. Castle was, however, socked in by the thick tule fog common in California's Central Valley in the winter, so all three aircraft set down at March AFB—within two minutes of the scheduled arrival time—after forty-five hours and nineteen minutes in the air.

LeMay personally awarded each crewman with a Distinguished Flying Cross for their "demonstration of SAC's capabilities to strike any target on the face of the earth."

The National Aeronautic Association awarded the year's Mackay Trophy to the 93rd Bombardment Wing for the flight, and it was a cover story for the glossy picture magazines.

According to *Time* magazine on January 28, "The momentous trip, announced the happy LeMay with transparent modesty, was 'just another training mission, no different from dozens and dozens of others.' In some ways, this was true. The crews were as carefully briefed and seemingly as routinely inured as for any long-distance trip. Yet as they proved once again SAC's enormous everyday striking power, it was also clear that SAC's able flyers had made the kind of history that would soar to the top of man's unending catalogue of conquests over nature."

"Did Russia know of the mission?" LeMay was asked by a reporter.

"Certainly, Russia knew about it," replied the general.

So, too, apparently, did Congress.

A few weeks later, on March 11, *Time* reported that "at a press conference, Secretary of Defense Wilson vaguely remarked that production of the B-52 intercontinental bomber might soon 'be up for reconsideration,'" but, when Boeing stock fell 3.5 points, "the Air Force hastily announced that Boeing had firm orders for 502 B-52 bombers [and] that its present orders will keep it busy for at least three years."

While Kick Start and Power Flite were designed for publicity, they served as prototypes of B-52 operations that proceeded without much notice through the middle period of the Cold War and that were designed to demonstrate SAC's "capabilities to strike any target on the face of the earth."

Operationally, it was not top secret that the mission of the Strategic Air Command B-52 force was to be prepared to launch a nuclear counterstrike against the Soviet Union within a moment's notice of any indication of a Soviet strike being launched against the United States. Essentially, it would be the same application of strategic air power that had been used against Germany and Japan—but launched immediately and with nuclear weapons.

To execute their mission, B-52s were placed on alert at SAC bases on the northern tier of the United States, as well as flying airborne alert missions. These airborne alert missions were flown under a variety of operational names. For example, Operation Coverall was an airborne alert over the Atlantic Ocean, and Operation Chrome Dome—initiated in 1960 and kept secret for its first year—called for Stratofortresses to be on airborne alert patrols near the Soviet Union at all times.

Another ongoing secret SAC B-52 mission was code-named Hard Head. Initiated in 1961, Hard Head involved observing the Ballistic Missile Early Warning System (BMEWS) radar facility at Thule AB in Greenland, which, in turn, was designed to watch for potential Soviet missile launches. The Thule Monitor Missions, as Hard Head was also known, maintained visual surveillance of the radar site so that if the North American Aerospace Defense Command (NORAD) ever lost contact with Thule, it could be determined whether or not the Thule site had been destroyed in an act of war.

Under Chrome Dome, a dozen Stratofortresses, one from each of SAC's twelve wings, remained on

Gen. Curtis LeMay commanded the USAAF B-29 force in the Pacific during World War II, took over SAC in 1948, and commanded it for an unprecedented nine years. During that time, he built it into a highly disciplined force and the largest strategic nuclear force in the world. He later served as chief of staff of the U.S. Air Force. *USAF*

station for twenty-four hours somewhere in the world until it was relieved by another, so there were always at least a dozen B-52s on patrol. As Tom Power later observed, it was a defense strategy that "never has been attempted in the military history of the world before."

The routine, often alluded to in Cold War–era movies, involved the Combat Mission Folder in an orange box that was brought to the Stratofortress by the pilot and chained to the cockpit before each mission. It contained everything from maps to codes that would be necessary for arming the nuclear weapons and flying to a predetermined target within the Soviet Union.

The flights, which often covered more than 10,000 miles, were described by crews as "high-speed loitering," which kept them within striking distance of the Soviet Union, but involved no dramatic maneuvering that might increase fuel consumption rates. The twenty-four hours would be punctuated by aerial refuelings and rotating catnaps for the crews.

Meanwhile, overall command and control was maintained by the Boeing EC-135 Looking Glass flying command post electronic communications aircraft that flew their own continuous airborne patrols out of SAC headquarters at Offutt AFB in Nebraska. The flights were pared back to just four bombers after 1966 when SAC intercontinental ballistic missiles were deemed capable of providing a corresponding deterrent.

The Chrome Dome missions conjured up the ponderous and perilous reality of a Cold War with the Damocles sword of nuclear annihilation hanging over the heads of Americans and Soviets. However, Tom Power was not entirely obsessed with the somber. Like his mentor, LeMay, he enjoyed using a good long-distance flight to publicize the capabilities of his B-52s.

■ Brig. Gen. William Eubank, the 93rd Bombardment Wing commander, talks with Air Force officers on the flight line at Castle AFB after the first B-52 operational flight in June 1955.
USAF

Though Power Flite demonstrated virtually unlimited range with aerial refueling—and the KC-135 would soon make this routine—Tom Power was especially interested in showing how far a Stratofortress could fly *without* refueling. On September 26, 1958, two of the 28th Bombardment Wing's B-52Ds set world speed records of 560.7 miles per hour over a 10,000-kilometer course, and 597.7 miles per hour over a 5,000-kilometer course. On December 14, 1960, a 5th Bombardment Wing B-52G set a world distance record, flying 10,078.8 miles without refueling. The record stood for just over a year, until it was topped by a 4136th Strategic Wing B-52H flying unrefueled for 12,532.28 miles from Kadena AB on Okinawa to Torrejon AB in Spain. This record stood for twenty-four years until it was topped by the Rutan Voyager.

The SAC slogan is proclaimed on a billboard near the main gate of Offutt AFB during the LeMay era. *USAF*

While the Chrome Dome dozen were on station somewhere high over the arctic, Power had ordered a sizable proportion of the Strategic Air Command B-52 and KC-135 fleet to remain on ground alert status at bases across the northern tier of the United States. These included Fairchild AFB near Spokane, Glasgow AFB in Montana, Minot AFB and Grand Forks AFB in North Dakota, Ellsworth AFB in South Dakota, Sawyer AFB and Wurtsmith AFB in Michigan, Griffiss AFB in New York, and Loring AFB in Maine.

At these bases, SAC's aircrews remained in partially blast-proof bunkers on seven-day alert tours, ready to dash to their aircraft on a moment's notice and get their bombers airborne in fifteen minutes. In practice, many crews got from the bunker to engine-start in five minutes. When they did take off, the Stratofortress crews trained to do so as quickly as possible. The Minimum Interval Takeoff (MITO) involved whole squadrons of B-52s, as well as KC-135s, taking off twelve to fifteen seconds apart. It was a truly awe-inspiring spectacle that this author was privileged to behold.

In 1960, SAC opened the doors at Westover AFB to journalist Ed Rees for an article that appeared in *Time* magazine on March 14.

"In the act of reporting for alert duty, Lieutenant Colonel Dante Bulli and his crew in effect braced themselves at the end of a taut, outstretched spring," Rees writes colorfully. "The trigger was the rasping sound of a klaxon horn. At any moment, that horn might blow. It could mean that a Soviet nose cone was on its way carrying destruction, and that there were 15 minutes in which to get off the ground and head for preassigned Soviet targets. There would be no time for second thoughts, no room for second-guessing as to whether some button-pusher was running a test. To SAC alert crews, the klaxon is a cry to arms."

■ In January 1957, three B-52Bs of the 93rd Bombardment Wing departed from Castle AFB in California for Operation Power Flite, a record-setting round-the-world nonstop flight. It demonstrated that the United States had the ability to deliver a thermonuclear weapon anywhere in the world. *USAF*

■ The route taken by the Operation Power Flite B-52Bs. The 24,325 miles were completed in forty-five hours and nineteen minutes. *USAF*

■ Operation Power Flite succeeded in sending three B-52Bs around the world nonstop by using aerial refueling provided by KC-97G tankers. Within a few years, the slow KC-97Gs were entirely replaced by faster KC-135 jets. *USAF*

In fact, the crews were frequently subjected to drills, during which they were not told to stand down until they were ready to release their brakes and start down the runway, or until after they had completed their MITO.

"The only time you dare take a shower," one pilot told Rees, "is right after an alert. Some day they'll fool us and blow the horn again just after we get back."

Going MAD

In the early 1950s, as the United States and the Soviet Union were beginning to build up their stockpiles of nuclear weapons and the missiles and bombers to deliver them against one another, planners in both countries drafted their war plans with the assumption that they could be integrated into tactical doctrine.

As an arms race ensued during the decade, the number of weapons—to use an unavoidable pun—mushroomed. According to the *Bulletin of the Atomic Scientists*, the number in the United States arsenal grew from 235 in 1949, the year of the first Soviet test, to more than 15,000 in 1959. The Soviet Union, meanwhile, appeared to have at least a thousand, although Western analysts assumed a greater number. By this time, both sides came to an understanding that the destructive power was so great that nuclear weapons could never be part of an integrated battlefield doctrine involving a war between super-powers. Phrases such as "Armageddon" and "Doomsday Scenario" frequently cropped up when arsenals of these weapons were mentioned.

The only way that nuclear weapons could be used in a World War III between the United States and the Soviet Union would be as a final measure. The war for which Lt. Col. Dante Bulli and men like him trained would be the last war. It was generally believed that a full-blown nuclear exchange between the superpowers would so devastate the world that civilization itself would be obliterated. Albert Einstein, the great physicist whose famous 1939 letter to Franklin Roosevelt put the United States on the road to building the first nuclear weapon, famously quipped that after World War III was fought as a nuclear war, World War IV would be fought with "sticks and stones." The implication is clear.

While Einstein's characterization is more graphic, this notion of bilateral annihilation was coldly articulated as strategic policy by Robert McNamara. The Defense Secretary is widely remembered for being one of the first to articulate the policy of "Mutual Assured Destruction"—best known by its acronym MAD—the principle by which a nuclear power would not attempt the destruction of another for fear that it would be destroyed itself.

This was the template by which SAC's LGM-30 Minuteman ICBM force was built up in the 1960s. As McNamara explained in an interview with the National Security Archive of George Washington University aired on CNN in 1998, "Mutual Assured Destruction is the foundation of stable deterrence in a nuclear world. It's not mad, it's logical."

Broken Arrows and Other Problems

No discussion of the SAC Stratofortress during the era of the airborne nuclear alert is complete without mention of the "Broken Arrows" involving B-52s that crashed with nuclear weapons aboard. Though the term is commonly used to denote incidents involving aircraft, it actually encompasses a wider range of delivery systems. Indeed, most Broken Arrows reported since the 1960s involve submarines.

Technically, Broken Arrow specifically refers to any accidental event involving nuclear weapons that does not create the risk of nuclear war. According to U.S. Defense Department protocol, Broken Arrow is a subclassification of Pinnacle, which is a Joint Chiefs of Staff Operational Event/Incident Report (OPREP-3) "flagword" used within the National Command Authority reporting structure to identify "an incident of national or international interest and to provide time-sensitive information to commanders regarding any significant event that has occurred or is in progress."

While a number of Stratofortresses have been lost in crashes through the decades, several B-52 Broken Arrow incidents that took place during the 1960s are of note. The first of these occurred on January 24, 1961, when a B-52G carrying two Mk 39 (later W39) nuclear weapons crashed near Goldsboro, North Carolina. A major fuel leak was reported during a nighttime aerial refueling, and the aircraft became uncontrollable during an attempt at an emergency landing at Seymour-Johnson AFB. The crew ejected at 9,000 feet, and the bomber disintegrated before crashing.

Both weapons separated from the aircraft, with the descent of one being slowed by a parachute. The other weapon plowed into soft dirt and buried itself as deep as about 55 feet in the mud. Everything was recovered except the thermonuclear stage of the second weapon. This was left in place at the site, which was purchased by the government and fenced off to prevent tampering. There is still a controversy around the subject of how close the weapons came to exploding.

On March 14, less than two months after the Goldsboro incident, a B-52F out of Mather AFB in California suffered an uncontrolled decompression and was forced to fly below refueling altitude. Having run out of fuel, it crashed near Yuba City, California. The crew escaped, and the nuclear weapons were recovered.

Also important to mention while on the subject of B-52 accidents is a series that was the result of vertical stabilizers being lost in low altitude turbulence. These incidents occurred as SAC began low-level flight training to prepare crews for below-the-radar penetrations of Soviet air space.

Not all of these vertical stabilizer accidents involved nuclear weapons. A case in point was a B-52C of the 99th Bombardment Squadron, out of Westover AFB, Massachusetts, which was lost on January 24, 1963, coincidentally exactly two years after Goldsboro. Another coincidence is that the pilot of the aircraft was the same Lt. Col. Dante Bulli who had been interviewed at Westover by Ed Rees of *Time* magazine two years earlier. Bulli's aircraft lost its tail in severe turbulence while operating below 500 feet over Piscataquis

The wreckage of a B-52G lost in a January 1966 collision with a KC-135 over the Mediterranean lies strewn on a beach near Palomares, Spain, while a U.S. Navy ship stands offshore as part of the search for a missing nuclear weapon.

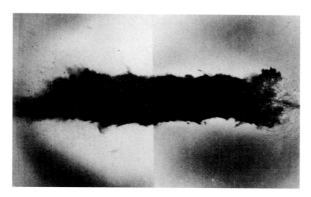

This aerial photograph shows the blackened ice field near Thule, Greenland, where a B-52G crashed in January 1968 while attempting an emergency landing. *USAF*

In January 1964, a B-52H piloted by Boeing test pilot Chuck Fisher lost its vertical stabilizer in severe turbulence over the Rockies. Amazingly, Fisher managed to land safely. *USAF*

County, Maine, and crashed into Elephant Mountain. Only Bulli, his copilot, and the navigator escaped the aircraft, but the copilot was killed when he impacted a tree. Seven other crewmen were killed in the crash.

Nearly a year later, a three-man Boeing crew suffered the loss of a vertical stabilizer on a test flight out of the company's facility in Wichita, but managed to save the aircraft. The January 10, 1964, mission had involved cruising at an altitude of 500 feet over the

Colorado Rockies, but when the B-52H encountered moderate turbulence, pilot Chuck Fisher climbed to 14,300 feet, where he briefly found smooth air. However, rough turbulence suddenly rocked the ship. It was jabbed from the side severely, then tossed up and down. The crew noted high vertical g-forces and lateral motion of the airplane.

As Fisher recalled, "I gave orders to prepare to abandon the airplane, because I didn't think we were going to keep it together. We didn't know what was damaged, but control was difficult. We cut our speed to 225 knots, and dropped to about 5,000 feet. Everybody was ready, should the need come to leave the ship. We figured we'd put a little more altitude between us and the ground, so we climbed to 16,000 feet very slowly. We kept trying to figure out the reason for our control problem. We had all eight engines, and all leading edges, but the plane would suddenly pitch or buck in response to control. When this happened, control was very marginal and we didn't hold out much hope for getting it in a landable condition."

Fisher attempted to return to Wichita, but the pilot of a Boeing chase plane who met him reported the loss of 90 percent of the vertical tail. Because of weather at Wichita and the large population in the area, Fisher diverted to Blytheville AFB in Arkansas, shadowed by several chase planes, including a KC-135 full of Boeing engineers. Six hours after the incident occurred, Fisher and his crew successfully landed the damaged

B-52H, demonstrating that the aircraft was at least *theoretically* flyable in this condition.

This also provided Boeing with information vital for retrofitting the Stratofortress fleet to head off later problems. This project, initiated at Boeing's Wichita facility with the Load Alleviation and Mode Stabilization (LAMS) study, led to development of an advanced flight control system.

Just three days after Fisher's accident, though, a similar incident did not end so happily. A B-52D returning to Georgia from a Chrome Dome deployment to Europe lost its vertical stabilizer in heavy turbulence over Pennsylvania and crashed into Savage Mountain near Cumberland, Maryland. Two of the four crewmembers who successfully ejected died of hypothermia before being rescued. According to a Defense Department summary, the two Mk 53 (later B53) nuclear weapons that had been aboard the bomber were found "relatively intact in the middle of the wreckage."

In the latter part of the decade, two well-publicized Stratofortress Broken Arrow incidents occurred overseas, in Spain and Greenland. Often considered to be the most serious of such accidents, they are also the only two events involving aircraft of any type that were on *Time* magazine's 2009 and 2011 "Worst Nuclear Disasters" lists.

The first of these occurred on January 17, 1966, with a B-52G based at Seymour-Johnson AFB in North Carolina that was on a Chrome Dome deployment. This aircraft collided with a KC-135 Stratotanker during a refueling operation at 31,000 feet over the Mediterranean Sea off the coast of Spain, near the fishing village of Palomares. The fuel load of the tanker exploded, killing all four crew members, while the Stratofortress broke up, killing three of the seven men aboard. Three of the four Mk 28 (later B28) thermonuclear weapons aboard the aircraft struck land near Palomares. According to SAC, two of these "underwent non-nuclear TNT-type explosions on impact," when they crashed on land, releasing "some radioactive material," specifically plutonium.

The fourth weapon fell into the Mediterranean, and was the subject of an extensive search involving a flotilla of U.S. Navy ships, including the recently commissioned deep-water submersible *Alvin*. The weapon was found unexploded on a 70-degree slope at a depth of 2,550 feet on March 17, but it took two attempts before it was successfully recovered on April 7.

On January 21, 1968, two years after Palomares, another B-52G crashed, this time on sea ice in North Star Bay, Greenland.

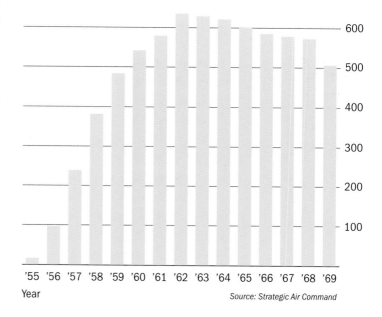

B-52s in the SAC Inventory: Buildup and Peak Strength Era

Numbers exclude aircraft not assigned to SAC

Year

Source: Strategic Air Command

The aircraft, assigned to the 380th Strategic Bombardment Wing at Plattsburgh AFB in New York, experienced a cabin fire while on an Operation Hard Head patrol over Baffin Bay and was attempting to make an emergency landing at Thule AB in Greenland. Six of the seven crew members managed to eject successfully, but the four Mk 28s aboard were scattered in the crash, and there were extensive radiation leaks.

The Project Crested Ice cleanup operation began immediately in an attempt to contain all of the nuclear material dispersed in a 3-square-mile debris field. This was complicated by high winds and bitterly cold temperatures, as well as the fact that the fire that consumed the Stratofortress had melted some of the ice, causing some wreckage and other material to go into the ocean. Most, though not all, of the bomb components had been recovered when Crested Ice was terminated in September.

The Thule incident created political embarrassment in Denmark, which owns Greenland, because the country had earlier declared itself a nuclear-free zone. This furor in international relations caused by both Palomares and Thule accelerated a decision by the United States to stand down both Chrome Dome and Hard Head operations. The exact nature of the Hard Head missions, meanwhile, would not be revealed until much later.

Stand-Off Missiles, the First Generation

The Stratofortress had been conceived at a time when the primary method by which a bomber delivered ordnance was to drop bombs. During World War II, aircraft had been adapted to fire short-range rockets, which were mostly unguided and mostly used against ground targets. The use of long-range, air-dropped missiles against strategic targets was the subject of various studies in the 1940s, but it was not until the late 1950s that the U.S. Air Force seriously planned to use the Stratofortress to carry such missiles.

The catalyst for this change of tactics was the growing threat presented by an increasingly sophisticated Soviet air defense system. Originally, it was assumed that high-flying postwar bombers would operate at altitudes that would make them immune to antiaircraft fire. However, by the mid-1950s, advances in surface-to-air missiles caused strategic planners on both sides of the Iron Curtain to do some rethinking.

Strategic missiles carried by bombers are called stand-off weapons for a good reason. They allow the bomber to release its ordnance a safe distance from a heavily defended target, then turn and flee. They also allow the bomber to be farther from the blast of its own thermonuclear weapon. A variety of missiles were considered and tested. For example, the Bell B-63 (later GAM-63) Rascal was test launched from the B-47. The first one to be widely deployed as B-52 armament was the North American GAM-77 (later AGM-28) Hound Dog air-launched cruise missile.

The Air Force initiated the Hound Dog project in early 1959 with the first guided, air-launched flight test of the XGAM-77 prototype coming in August, and deliveries of operational missiles by year end. Inertially guided and turbojet-propelled, each missile

■ An artist's conception of an AGM-28 Hound Dog, marked with the SAC shield, headed for its target. A Stratofortress can be seen banking away in the distance.

■ Left: A B-52G armed with two AGM-28 Hound Dogs on its underwing pylons. For many years after the Hound Dog was introduced, these pylons were referred to as AGM-28 pylons, whether they held other types of missiles or gravity bombs. The pylons could each accommodate a dozen Mk 82 bombs and did so during the Vietnam War. *USAF* ■ Right: A B-52G armed with four XGAM-87A (later AGM-48) Skybolts. The missile represented a state of the art in long range stand-off weaponry that was not to be matched again for two decades with the AGM-86. *USAF*

carried a W28 thermonuclear warhead. They were 42 feet 6 inches long and weighed 10,000 pounds.

Hound Dogs could be launched nearly 800 miles from the target, allowing the B-52 to turn for home before they struck the target. Hound Dogs deployed quickly, reaching a peak inventory of 593 AGM-28As in service with SAC by 1963. Eventually, nearly 500 missiles were modified to have a smaller radar cross section and redesignated as the AGM-28B.

Many B-52Gs, as well as some examples of all models back to the B-52C, were retrofitted to carry the Hound Dog. Such modifications included strengthening the wing and adding underwing pylons between the inboard engine and the fuselage so that each bomber could carry a pair of Hound Dogs.

Simultaneous with the development of the Hound Dog was that of the McDonnell GAM-72 (later ADM-20) Quail, a missile whose function was to act as a decoy by emulating the Stratofortress on radar. Though it had the same radar signature as a B-52 bomber, it actually resembled a large winged refrigerator in size and shape. The Quail's autopilot could be preprogrammed for a flight path simulating that of a bomber, and an infrared device aboard mimicked the heat signature of a bomber's engines.

In the early 1950s, the U.S. Air Force had started looking into developing self-propelled decoys that could be carried aboard bombers such as the B-36 and B-47, which were tasked potentially with flying missions into Soviet air space. Of the decoys designed, only the Quail was deployed. The first test flight of a powered Quail occurred in August 1958 after glide tests beginning late in 1957.

The Quail entered service with SAC units in early 1961, being flown mainly aboard B-52Gs and B-52Hs. With their wings folded, eight Quails could be accommodated in a B-52 bomb bay, though operationally, the bombers carried fewer. Redesignated as ADM-20 in 1963, more than five hundred Quails were delivered. They remained in service until 1978, by which time radar technology had improved to the point where the Soviets could distinguish real bombers from Quails.

Other steps that were taken in the 1950s to address the Soviet air defense threat included both tactics and electronics. In considering the former, mission planners instituted low-level attack scenarios in which the bombers would fly under Soviet radar before launching their missiles. Indeed, the intended launch scenario for the Hound Dog was at low level.

As noted earlier, terrain avoidance systems were introduced as standard in the B-52E and B-52F, retrofitted into earlier B-52s, and included in later models as they were delivered. Strengthened airframes were also part of the preparation for low-level operations, as were electronic countermeasures (ECM) packages designed to protect the bombers from Soviet missiles, early warning radar, and ground control intercept radar.

Even as the Hound Dog was becoming operational, the U.S. Air Force had even higher hopes for a strategic missile with nearly twice the range. The Douglas GAM-87

■ An August 1961 view of a Douglas XGAM-87A (later AGM-48) Skybolt on its hydraulic loading trailer, parked next to a Stratofortress.

■ Frames from a grainy 16mm film of an XGAM-87A (later AGM-48) Skybolt being test fired from a Stratofortress. This may be film of the first successful launch on December 19, 1962. Ironically, this was the same day as the program's termination. *USAF*

(later AGM-48) Skybolt was developed in the late 1950s at a time when ICBMs were still liquid-fueled, cumbersome to launch, and not yet fully reliable. The Skybolt was powered by a solid-fuel rocket engine, weighed 11,000 pounds, and, at 38 feet and 3 inches, was more compact than a Hound Dog. It was designed so that four could be carried by a single Stratofortress, and it was once intended that the Skybolt would be the principal armament of the B-52H.

As the Skybolt was being developed for the U.S. Air Force and showing great promise as a Stratofortress-launched weapon, it also attracted the attention of the British. Seeking to maintain their own independent, state-of-the art nuclear strike capability, the British agreed in May 1960 to adopt the Skybolt and hang it on their Avro Vulcan bombers. In so doing, they abandoned a plan to improve Avro's own Blue Steel stand-off missile.

The British commitment notwithstanding, Defense Secretary Robert McNamara had grown cool on the Skybolt concept because of unsuccessful test launches and the promise of the upcoming Minuteman solid-fuel ICBM. This set the stage for a headline-grabbing political crisis that would nearly bring down the British government and that damaged Anglo-American relations for years.

The Skybolt was first successfully air launched on December 19, 1962—the same day that McNamara chose to cancel the program. The night before, at a meeting in the Bahamas, President John F. Kennedy had told British Prime Minister Harold MacMillan that the ax was about to fall. As a consolation, Kennedy allowed MacMillan to acquire the Polaris SLBM for the Royal Navy's submarines, which was arguably a better operational choice for the British.

For the Strategic Air Command, this meant that the service life of the Hound Dog would be extended until 1977. It would be two decades before the AGM-86 Air-Launched Cruise Missile (ALCM) finally filled the gap left by the Skybolt cancellation.

Senior Bowl

Kept in strictest secrecy at the time, two B-52Hs were configured in the late 1960s to carry unmanned reconnaissance aircraft on their underwing pylons. This was the Mach-3-plus Lockheed D-21 drone, which was originally designed to be launched from the M-21 "Mothership" variant of the Mach-3-plus Lockheed SR-71 Blackbird manned reconnaissance aircraft. Like the Blackbird, the D-21 was conceived by Kelly Johnson's Advanced Research Projects department at Lockheed, known as the Skunk Works. The idea for each was an aircraft too fast for any other aircraft to catch and that could therefore operate with impunity in any hostile airspace.

Powered by Marquardt RJ43 ramjet engines, the D-21 was just a few inches longer than a Hound Dog at 42 feet 10 inches long, with a wingspan of 19 feet. Its range once launched from the mothership would exceed 3,000 miles.

The D-21 was designed to be recovered by parachute after it ejected a module containing sensor gear, its reconnaissance camera, and film exposed on its mission. First launched in March 1966, the D-21 suffered a failure on its fourth flight that resulted in the loss of both drone and mothership. In the wake of this incident, Kelly Johnson proposed that they switch to using a B-52H as the mothership. The launch would be at subsonic speeds, but the D-21 could be *under* the mothership, and hence it could be *dropped* rather than having to be launched from the top of another aircraft. Under the operational name Senior Bowl, the first successful launch of a D-21 from a B-52H occurred in June 1968.

Between November 1969 and March 1971, B-52Hs flying out of Andersen AFB on Guam launched four D-21s in unsuccessful attempts to observe the Chinese nuclear test site at Lop Nor. These failures, combined with advances in satellite technology, resulted in the termination of Senior Bowl, though its existence was not revealed until 1977.

■ A B-52H carrying a pair of Mach-3-plus Lockheed D-21B reconnaissance drones. This configuration was used operationally between November 1969 and March 1971. *USAF*

Balls Eight

During the 1950s, aviation technology was moving by leaps and bounds. Aircraft were establishing new speed and altitude records by substantial margins and doing so routinely. In the United States, Edwards AFB in California was the center of the action during the heyday of the quest for higher and faster. By 1959, North American Aviation had developed the ultimate expression of the era, the X-15. This aircraft was destined to set records that still stand today. It is still the fastest powered, winged, and manned aircraft ever flown. (The Space Shuttle reentered the atmosphere at higher speeds, but it was unpowered at this stage.)

The first of three X-15 aircraft was originally delivered in U.S. Air Force markings, but the program was managed jointly by the U.S. Air Force and NASA, with pilots from both entities, as well as the U.S. Navy, participating in the program's 199 flights. Like other manned and unmanned research aircraft before and since, the X-15 was designed to be air-launched rather than runway-launched.

As a carrier aircraft, the B-52 Stratofortress was uniquely suited to the task. It had the payload capacity, and the high wing meant that an aircraft could be accommodated on a pylon beneath the wing, as were the unmanned Hound Dog or Skybolt.

The X-15 was 50 feet 9 inches long and weighed around 17 tons when launched, triple the weight of the Hound Dog or Skybolt. Therefore, the Stratofortress was the

■ The X-24A lifting-body research aircraft begins its rocket-powered flight after being launched from the wing of NASA's NB-52B mothership during a 1970 research flight. *NASA*

■ One of three X-15 rocket-powered research aircraft being carried aloft under the wing of its NB-52A mothership. The X-15 was air-launched from the Stratofortress so the rocket plane would have enough fuel to reach its high speed and altitude test points. *NASA*

■ High-altitude contrails frame the NB-52A mothership as it carries the X-15 aloft for Air Force Major Robert White's first X-15 flight in April 1960. *NASA*

NASA's NB-52B lifts off on August 1, 1997, carrying the X-38 lifting body, then being considered as a prototype for an emergency crew return vehicle for the International Space Station. *NASA*

A Space Shuttle Solid Rocket Booster Drop Test Vehicle (SRB-DTV) captive flight aboard the NB-52B on June 10, 1977. *NASA*

The NB-52E testbed, the second B-52E to be built, was diverted from operational service and used for a series of special test programs. *USAF*

The first X-43A hypersonic research aircraft and its modified Pegasus booster rocket are carried by NASA's NB-52B from Dryden Flight Research Center at Edwards AFB on June 2, 2001. *NASA photo, Tony Landis*

only aircraft that could realistically function in this role, and even then a 48-square-foot section of the right wing flap had to be cut out to accommodate the X-15 tail.

In 1958 and 1959, two Stratofortresses were assigned as carrier aircraft. The first was the third of the three B-52As, tail number 52-0003. The second was the fourth RB-52B, tail number 52-0008. When given a permanent status as test aircraft, the two aircraft were redesignated as NB-52A and NB-52B. The NB-52A received the dramatic official name *The High and Mighty One*, while the NB-52B went unnamed, but came to be known, by its 0008 tail number, as *Balls Eight*. The NB-52A was retired in 1969, but *Balls Eight* went on to serve for an additional 35 years, until 2004.

The High and Mighty One made its first flight with the X-15 attached on March 10, 1959, and the first flight in which the X-15 was air-dropped for a glide test came on June 8. The first powered flight of the X-15 was on September 17. *Balls Eight* carried the X-15 for the first time on January 23, 1960 in the fifth flight of the X-15 program. Over the next eight years, the NB-52B carried the X-15s for most their 199 flights, as well as several "captive" flights in which the rocket plane was carried but not launched. During the program, the X-15 established a speed record of 4,520 miles per hour (Mach 6.72) and an altitude record of 354,330 feet.

◼ An aerial view showing Stratofortresses on the flight line at Loring AFB, near the town of Limestone, Maine. *U.S. Geological Survey*

■ The tall tails of a group of SAC RB-52B aircraft. *USAF*

Members of a SAC B-52 combat crew race for their always ready-and-waiting Stratofortress. Fifty percent of the SAC bomber and tanker force were on continuous ground alert. *USAF*

Even before the last flight of the X-15 on October 24, 1968, both of the Stratofortress motherships were being used to air drop other research aircraft. These included the lifting bodies, which studied how virtually wingless aircraft used their fuselage to produce lift. The tests evaluated the flight characteristics of such aircraft, which were seen as a potentially useful design for craft reentering the earth's atmosphere from outer space.

The specific lifting body aircraft tested in the 1960s and 1970s included Northrop's M2-F2/F3 and HL-10, as well as Martin Marietta's X-24A and X-24B. The M2-F2 made its first glide test on July 12, 1966, followed by that of the HL-10 on December 22. The M2-F2 made sixteen flights, all but four with *Balls Eight*, which carried the aircraft twenty-seven times after it was rebuilt as the M2-F3. The HL-10 made thirty-seven flights through December 1972, eleven of them with the NB-52A and the rest with *Balls Eight*.

Balls Eight carried the X-24A on its first glide test on April 17, 1969, and for twenty-six of its twenty-eight flights, including all the powered flights in 1970 and 1971. The aircraft was rebuilt, redesignated as X-24B, and carried by *Balls Eight* on its first glide test on August 1, 1973, as well as its first powered flight on November 15. After thirty-six flights, including six glide tests, the X-24B made its last powered flight on September 9,

1975. This flight marked the end of manned flight involving rocket-propelled aircraft at Edwards AFB, but not the end of the career of the NB-52B.

After having been the mothership for 127 of the 144 lifting body flights, *Balls Eight* went on to work with a series of unmanned research aircraft programs, such as the Drones for Aerodynamic and Structural Testing (DAST) program. During 1977–1978 and 1983–1985, *Balls Eight* was also used in the development of the parachute recovery system that was used for the Space Shuttle's solid rocket boosters (SRBs). In 1983, it was used in the highly maneuverable aircraft technology (HiMAT) project. The NB-52B was then used for a 1990 series of eight tests of the drag chute system that was to be installed on the Space Shuttle Orbiters and first used by it in May 1992.

Beginning on April 5, 1990, *Balls Eight* served as the mothership on the first six flights of the Orbital Sciences Corporation's Pegasus rocket boosters.

At the end of the century, NASA and *Balls Eight* returned to the lifting body concept for the X-38 program. The X-38 aircraft were a series of prototype research vehicles designed to develop the technology to build and operate a Crew Return Vehicle (CRV), or "lifeboat," for emergency use by the crews of the International Space Station. The X-38 was an unmanned craft similar in size and appearance to the X-24A.

The debut test flight of an X-38 atmospheric test vehicle was air-launched by *Balls Eight* on March 12, 1998, with NASA touting it as a first step toward "the first reusable human spacecraft to be built in more than two decades." Though subsequent flight tests were successful, the program was cancelled in April 2002 for budgetary reasons, nine years before the Space Shuttle, the only other reusable human spacecraft, was permanently grounded.

The career of the NB-52B ended on a high note as the mothership for NASA's Hyper-X program. Developed by NASA in cooperation with Boeing, MicroCraft Inc., Orbital Sciences Corporation, and the General Applied Science Laboratory (GASL), the Hyper-X aircraft was an unmanned hypersonic vehicle designated as X-43A. The goal of Hyper-X was to accumulate research data for a possible future high-speed, single-stage-to-orbit, manned spaceplane.

After launch from the mothership, the X-43A was powered to its operational altitude by a modified Pegasus first stage booster rocket, where the booster was

Gen. Curtis LeMay (center), flanked by Maj. Gen. Robert Terrill and Col. E. M. Nichols, at SAC headquarters. *USAF*

Gen. Thomas Power succeeded Curtis LeMay as commander of SAC in 1957. He served until 1964, presiding over SAC when it was at its peak B-52 strength. *SAC*

released and a scramjet engine took over. Though the first flight in June 2001 ended in failure, the second, in March 2004, established the X-43 as the fastest air-breathing (jet-propelled) aircraft ever flown. The third flight, on November 16, 2004, set a speed record of 7,546 miles per hour (Mach 9.8).

A month later, *Balls Eight* was formally retired from active service with NASA on December 17, 2004, destined for replacement by the NB-52H (see Chapter 12). As the NASA press release noted, it had "participated in some of the most significant projects in aerospace history. At retirement, the air launch and research aircraft held the distinction of being NASA's oldest aircraft, as well as being the oldest B-52 on flying status. At the same time, it had the lowest number of flying hours (2,443.8) of any B-52 in operation."

"At the time [it came off the production line on June 11, 1955], I'd wager, no one could have conceived that this airplane would have a remarkable 49-and-a-half-year career," observed Air Force historian James Young. "In fact, several times during that span of those 49 years there were many people who said its service life was over."

The Other Research Stratofortresses

The two motherships were not the only Stratofortresses diverted from SAC for research programs. One of the others was the NB-52E (56-0632), which was used in the Load Alleviation and Mode Stabilization (LAMS) program, which was conducted in around 1966–1968 in response to the rash of vertical stabilizer losses suffered by Stratofortresses in low-altitude turbulence.

According to Boeing's P. M. Burris and M. A. Bender, in their report on the topic, this study demonstrated "the capabilities of an advanced flight control system (FCS) to alleviate gust loads and control structural modes on a large flexible aircraft using existing aerodynamic control surfaces as force producers. . . The FCS was designed to alleviate structural loads while flying through atmospheric turbulence. . . . [NB-52E] modifications included the addition of hydraulically powered controls, a fly-by-wire

The first of sixty-nine Wichita-built B-52D Stratofortresses, resplendent in Strategic Air Command markings. *USAF*

(FBW) pilot station, associated electronics and analog computers at the test engineer's stations, instrumentation for system evaluation, and the LAMS flight controller."

While the N prefix redesignation denotes a permanent reassignment to research work, several Stratofortresses were reassigned temporarily and redesignated with a J prefix. One RB-52B (52-0004), called *Tender Trap*, became a JB-52B in 1955, when it was used to study the results of the Operation Redwing thermonuclear tests in the Pacific. One JB-52C (53-0399) was used for various test projects by the Aeronautical Systems Division at Wright-Patterson AFB, while another JB-52C was retained for testing by Boeing in Wichita.

Several JB-52G aircraft (including 57-6470, 57-6473, 57-6477, 58-0159, and 58-0182) were assigned to the Air Armament Center at Eglin AFB in Florida for testing a variety of weapons and electronics systems, including the GAM-87 Skybolt missile. Another JB-52G, known as the Snowbird because it was painted overall gloss white, was used at Edwards AFB during the early testing of the AGM-86 Air-Launched Cruise Missile.

Meanwhile, a number of JB-52Hs (including 60-0003, 60-0004, 60-0005, and 60-0023) were used for weapons tests, including the Skybolt, as well as electronics systems tests, such as those of the AN/ASQ-38 bombing-navigation system.

THE STRATEGIC DOCTRINE most closely associated with Defense Secretary Robert McNamara is that of Mutual Assured Destruction (MAD). However, his tenure in this post—throughout most of the 1960s—is also inextricably intertwined with the United States' involvement in the war in Southeast Asia. He was present at the beginning, and he presided over both the escalation of it into America's biggest war in the second half of the twentieth century and over the faltering attempts by Lyndon Johnson to deescalate and conclude it.

While MAD became McNamara's signature strategic policy, he is less well known for the equally significant concept of Sublimited War. As he wrote in a September 5, 1961, memo to military department secretaries, he viewed the creation of a Military Assistance Command in South Vietnam (MACV) as "a laboratory for the development of improved organizational and operational procedures for conducting sublimited war."

In testimony before the Senate Armed Services Committee in 1961, McNamara defined this category of conflicts as being warfare in which "the scale and character of the hostilities are kept just below the threshold where the world would recognize it as overt military aggression." This was the initial step into a war that defined the United States for a generation, but one that McNamara viewed merely as peripheral. The prevailing beef in the American defense establishment at the time was that large-scale wars short of a full-scale conflict—which MAD existed to prevent—were a thing of the past. Future conventional wars, McNamara insisted, would be sublimited wars.

In 1961, U.S. Army Special Forces were sent into South Vietnam to help train the South Vietnamese in the conduct of sublimited war against the Viet Cong guerrillas, who were supported by Communist North Vietnam—and who did not view the war as sublimited. McNamara's dilemma was that the war could not be won if it *remained* sublimited. The service chiefs, whose job it was to *win* wars, suggested that the war should be won. By now, the former SAC commander, Gen. Curtis LeMay, was Chief of Staff of the Air Force. He advocated a concentrated strategic air offensive against North Vietnam to end the war at the enemy's source of supply.

Nevertheless, Secretary McNamara and the chairman of the Joint Chiefs of Staff, U.S. Army Gen. Maxwell Taylor, were adamant that the war should be fought exclusively in the South *after* enemy

■ "Casper The Friendly Ghost," a B-52F-70-BW from the 320th Bombardment Wing, dropping Mk 117 750-pound bombs over South Vietnam in 1965. *USAF*

■ Below: Secretary of Defense Robert McNamara discusses a "sublimited war" gotten out of hand at a White House cabinet meeting in November 1967. *DoD*

A camouflaged B-52D on the ramp at Andersen AFB on Guam. *Bill Yenne*

supplies had been delivered. Their view that air power should remain at a tactical, rather than strategic, level prevailed. Nobody could have imagined that they were setting the tone for a far-from-sublimited war that would still entangle America a dozen years later.

American involvement ratcheted up past the point of no return in August 1964, when North Vietnamese patrol boats attacked the U.S. Navy destroyer USS *Maddox* in the Gulf of Tonkin off the North Vietnamese coast. A second encounter reported two days later was subsequently determined to have been a false alarm based on faulty radar data, but the die was cast. The Gulf of Tonkin incident opened the door to the use of American tactical air power against targets in North Vietnam. In August, Congress authorized President Johnson to order retaliatory strikes by carrier-based tactical aircraft, and, on February 14, 1965, a full-fledged tactical air campaign began. Known as Operation Rolling Thunder, it involved both U.S. Navy and U.S. Air Force aircraft, and lasted, off-and-on, until 1968. Where once the strategy had been to allow the enemy to bring materiel into South Vietnam, now the effort was made at cutting supply lines.

The Strategic Air Command entered the Vietnam War (also called the War in Southeast Asia because of the ongoing air operations, and periodic ground operations, in neighboring Laos and Cambodia) in a support role. The U.S. Air Force had designated SAC as the single manager of all KC-135 air-refueling operations, so SAC was tasked with providing tanker support for fighter and other aircraft operated by all other major U.S. Air Force commands, including those operating in Southeast Asia.

Arc Light

At the same time, the Defense Department began drafting plans to use B-52s in Vietnam—but *not* in a strategic role against targets in North Vietnam. The idea was to use the ultimate strategic bomber against suspected hideouts of the Viet Cong insurgents in the jungles of South Vietnam. The capacity for carrying conventional ordnance, which had been secondary in the development of the Stratofortress as a weapons system, was now in the forefront.

This operation, code-named Arc Light, received the personal attention and approval of President Johnson. The Arc Light missions, flown from Andersen AFB on Guam, were originally to have included B-47s as well as B-52s, but the former were cut from the roster due to their shorter range.

The much-discussed, and widely reported, first combat mission involving B-52s came on June 18, 1965, with twenty-seven B-52Fs of the 7th and 320th Bombardment Wings attacking a supposed Viet Cong concentration at Ben Cat, just 33 miles north of Saigon. According to intelligence reports, the target held four battalions of Viet Cong, but a post-strike investigation found tunnels that had been used by the Viet Cong, but no casualties.

It was an inauspicious beginning. While en route, however, two of the Stratofortresses were lost in a midair collision on a refueling track. The incident was blamed on bad weather, poor planning, and an ill-advised decision to run the entire mission under radio silence. The Strategic Air Command History Office publication, *Activity Input to Project Corona Harvest, Arc Light*, observes that in 1965, "the concept of operational

In the early days of Arc Light operations, the Stratofortresses, such as the three B-52Ds seen here, flew in close formation for maximum effect on concentrated areas.

An Arc Light strike disintegrates a Viet Cong encampment and staging area approximately 30 miles northeast of Saigon on November 20, 1967.
USAF

A pair of B-52Ds approaches their Arc Light target north of Saigon in South Vietnam.
USAF

bombing procedures for large scale non-nuclear strikes was inconsistent with existing SAC materiel concepts," because Stratofortress crew training and doctrine had been designed for strategic nuclear missions.

Meanwhile, the American media considered the use of B-52s to be overkill. John Correll of *Air Force Magazine* credits *Time* magazine with coining the phrase "killing gnats with a sledgehammer." Other commentators substituted fleas and other small insects. In its June 25, 1965, issue, *Time* reported that "In hindsight, use of the B-52s had been an expensive means of hunting guerrillas, and the scheme's only real merit may well have been psychological. Hanoi could hardly fail to notice how quickly and easily SAC's huge squadrons had been brought into the Viet Nam battle. The B-52s would, of course, be enormously effective if turned onto the cities or factories of the north. But the jungle strike also served to prove once again that the war in South Viet Nam can be won only by foot soldiers, closely supported by tactical air strikes."

Nevertheless, after standing down for about a month, the Arc Light force resumed the attacks. Through the end of 1965, Guam-based B-52Fs of the 7th, 320th, and 454th Bombardment Wings flew over one hundred missions to Vietnam. Most of these were simply saturation bombing, but in the fall the B-52s turned to direct tactical support missions, backing the U.S. Marine Corps' Operation Harvest Moon and the U.S. Army First Cavalry operations in the Ia Drang Valley. Initially, the typical weapons load consisted of forty-two M117 750-pound bombs loaded internally and twenty-four 500-pound Mk 82s loaded externally.

As the Arc Light missions became routine, the Joint Chiefs of Staff designated "free bomb zones" where missions could be flown without any prior approval from the office of U.S. Army General William Westmoreland, commander of American forces in Vietnam. These zones were located in the southern Mekong Delta, north of Saigon and southeast of Da Nang. It also became routine to fly more frequent missions with smaller numbers of B-52s.

When Arc Light began, SAC had committed its fleet of B-52Fs, the newest of the high-tailed first-generation Stratofortresses, while reserving the B-52G and B-52H aircraft for the nuclear alert mission. Because Arc Light missions were often flown at night, the B-52Fs had their gloss white undersides repainted in gloss black.

Meanwhile, in December 1965, SAC's B-52D fleet began undergoing a $30.6 million High-Density Bombing System modification program nicknamed "Big Belly," which increased their bomb bay capacity from twenty-seven to eighty-four 500-pound conventional bombs, with provisions for another twenty-four on underwing pylons. This increased the bomb-carrying capacity of the B-52D to up to 60,000 pounds, compared

A definite pattern of bomb craters are left after an Arc Light "softening-up raid" in support of Operation Junction City in Tay Ninh Province, South Vietnam on March 10, 1967. *USAF*

U.S. Army troops make their way through a forest turned to burnt matchsticks by an Arc Light strike, circa 1967. *U.S. Army*

An airman guides a B-52D out of its revetment. The bases in Thailand were no more than an hour or two mission time from most Arc Light targets, while missions out of Guam could last twelve hours. *USAF*

with the 43,500 typically carried by the B-52F. In March and April 1966, these aircraft began arriving in Guam to replace the B-52Fs, which were gradually withdrawn.

The B-52Ds were painted with gloss-black undersides and vertical tail, while their upper sides were painted in the newly standardized Southeast Asia camouflage scheme, consisting of tan plus two shades of green.

In wartime, it has occasionally been suggested that a sign of having truly "made it" comes with being tarred with an off-color nickname. It was around this time that the B-52 joined this club, receiving one of those monikers of self-deprecating endearment that comes along from time to time with certain airplanes. In the lexicon of the crews that have come to know and love them the F-105 Thunderchief is known universally as "Thud," the F-111 as the "Aardvark," and the UH-1 Iroquois helicopter as "Huey." The A-10 Thunderbolt II will always be the "Warthog."

Dubbed Stratofortress by its manufacturer, the B-52 now became the "BUFF," an acronym for the less-repeatable nickname "Big Ugly Fat Fucker." In polite company, and in official U.S. Air Force fact sheets, the acronym is deciphered as the milder "Big Ugly Fat *Fellow.*"

The first B-52 missions into North Vietnam came on April 12 and 26, 1966, as the Stratofortresses struck Mu Gia Pass. Located about 65 miles south of the North Vietnamese city of Vinh, the pass was an important choke point on the Ho Chi Minh Trail supply route that funneled materiel to the Viet Cong. By 1966, the effectiveness of

Arc Light had improved considerably. Because they flew too high to be seen or heard until too late, B-52s were gradually becoming one of the weapons most dreaded by the Viet Cong. According to the official history of the Strategic Air Command, General Westmoreland told Air Force Chief of Staff John McConnell that "we know, from talking to many prisoners and defectors, that the enemy troops fear B-52s, tactical air, artillery, and armor. . . in that order."

This assertion was confirmed by Viet Cong documents captured in March 1966 during Operation Silver City II by the 173rd Airborne Battalion. Referencing these, John Schlight writes in *A Chronology of Important Airpower Events in Southeast Asia*, that "there was some evidence of reluctance [by enemy forces] of performing missions for fear of B-52 aircraft."

One of the most colorful first hand Viet Cong accounts of the experience of suffering through Arc Light raids comes from Truong Nhu Tang. The Minister of Justice for the Viet Cong, he wrote vividly about Arc Light in his 1985 book, *A Viet Cong Memoir*.

"It seemed, as I strained to press myself into the bunker floor, that I had been caught in the Apocalypse," Truong remembered. "The terror was complete. One lost control of bodily functions as the mind screamed incomprehensible orders to get out."

By June 1966, after a year in the war zone, B-52s, flying both day and night and in all kinds of weather, were dropping 8,000 tons of bombs monthly in Arc Light missions over South Vietnam. More than 5,000 B-52 Arc Light sorties were flown in 1966, and the number nearly doubled to around 9,700 in 1967.

This increase was made possible by an agreement with the government of Thailand in early 1967 to begin basing American aircraft at Thai military air bases, such as Udorn Royal Thai Air Force Base and U-Tapao Royal Thai Navy Airfield. The latter became a B-52 basing location in April 1967, and major Stratofortress operations continued here through the end of the war. The trips from Guam to South Vietnam were a 5,200-mile, 12-hour round trip for the BUFFs, but from U-Tapao, it was an hour or so, putting much less strain on aerial refueling assets.

Typically, B-52 missions would originate at Andersen and recover at U-Tapao. The aircraft would then fly around eight missions in and out of U-Tapao before returning to Guam for scheduled maintenance, which was unavailable in Thailand until after 1970. Other B-52 missions were also flown from Kadena AB on Okinawa, but these were unpublicized because of concerns about civil unrest on the island. Meanwhile, there was no effort made to conceal SAC KC-135 tanker operations, which were ongoing at Kadena throughout the War in Southeast Asia.

Over South Vietnam, the strike missions were directed by way of ground radar stations located throughout the country, and equipped with the AN/MSQ-77 Skyspot Ground Directed Bombing (GDB) system.

A notable use of Arc Light B-52s came during the defense of American forces at Khe Sanh in 1968, a battle that developed into the largest and most significant tactical air campaign yet seen in Southeast Asia. The BUFFs operated around the clock, arriving over the target in groups of up to six every few hours, guided by Skyspot, and capable of revising their targets with two hours notice.

During this operation, code-named Niagara, B-52s dropped 75,631 tons of bombs in 2,707 sorties. Nearly six hundred of these were a mere 300 yards from the American perimeter, but no Americans were hit. The attacks helped break the siege on Khe Sanh and forced the North Vietnamese to withdraw. One captured North Vietnamese

■ Touching down in Thailand. Stratofortresses were a familiar sight at Udorn Royal Thai Air Force Base and U-Tapao Royal Thai Navy Airfield. *USAF*

■ A B-52D, recently painted with its gloss black tail and undersurfaces. *USAF*

officer admitted that 75 percent of his regiment had been wiped one in just one Arc Light attack.

While Westmoreland said that "the thing that broke their back basically was the fire of the B-52s," Lyndon Johnson effused that it was "the most overwhelming, intelligent, and effective use of air power in the history of warfare."

In October 1968, shortly before the presidential election, Johnson terminated the Rolling Thunder campaign against North Vietnam north of the 20th parallel. However, the Arc Light missions in South Vietnam continued, as did B-52 participation in the Commando Hunt interdiction operations, aimed at segments of the North Vietnamese supply pipeline that ran through Laos. Indeed, the United States dropped more bombs on Laos during the war than on North Vietnam and more than half of the tonnage dropped in South Vietnam. Of all the Commando Hunt operations, B-52 operations were most heavily involved in Commando Hunt VII, between November 1971 and March 1972. These missions ranged from Laos, across North Vietnam to the port city of Vinh, and included Mu Gia Pass.

In 1969, the newly installed administration of Richard Nixon began making plans for American incursions into the North Vietnamese "sanctuaries" in Cambodia. These areas, adjacent to the heart of South Vietnam, had heretofore been off-limits to American attacks.

■ Secretary of State Dean Rusk, President Lyndon Johnson, and Secretary of Defense Robert McNamara at a meeting in the White House in February 1968, shortly after North Vietnam and the Viet Cong launched their Tet Offensive in South Vietnam. *DoD*

Beginning on March 18, B-52s were used against selected targets inside Cambodia. Because operations against the specific target areas were designated with code names such as Breakfast, Lunch, and Supper, the campaign came to be known as Menu. The missions, ordered directly by the president, were kept secret, even from many within the normal U.S. Air Force chain of command, and were not revealed to Congress until 1973. Arc Light missions were used as the "cover" for the B-52 participation in the covert Menu missions, which continued until May 1970 and accounted for 3,630 sorties dropping around 100,000 tons of ordnance.

In February and March 1971, BUFFs were used to back the ground incursion into North Vietnamese controlled areas of Laos by South Vietnamese troops—and to cover them during their subsequent retreat. B-52s flew 399 sorties in support of the former and 1,358 sorties in support of the latter.

Meanwhile, the number of Arc Light missions began a steady decline, based on a desire by the Nixon administration to "de-escalate" the unpopular war and turn the bulk of the ground fighting over to South Vietnam under a policy of "Vietnamization." In 1969, the number of Arc Light sorties, 19,498, was down slightly from the 1968 peak of 20,568, though still more than double the 1967 total of 9,686. In 1970 they fell to 15,103, and the next year, the number of sorties dropped to 12,552. By 1970, the long B-52 missions from Guam were phased out in favor of using only the bases in Thailand.

The control panel of a war-weary B-52D.
Bill Yenne

Linebacker

A turning point in the Southeast Asia air war came On March 30, 1972. Knowing that the United States was turning the conduct of the war over to South Vietnam, the North decided to test its southern neighbor with a robust escalation. The longtime reliance on the Viet Cong guerrillas with minimal North Vietnamese Army participation was superseded by a series of large-scale ground invasions, with regular army units supported by tanks and heavy artillery.

To meet this challenge, the U.S. Air Force's Pacific Air Forces command (PACAF) and U.S. Navy tactical airpower stepped up ground support operations, and large numbers of tactical aircraft were redeployed from bases in South Korea and the United States.

The halt to bombing operations against North Vietnam above the 20th parallel, which had been imposed by Lyndon Johnson more than three years before, was ended, and American air power went north once again under an air offensive designated as Operation Freedom Train. On April 9, as part of this effort, B-52s attacked Vinh, and six days later they struck petroleum and lubricant storage dumps near Haiphong, North Vietnam's largest port.

On May 8, Richard Nixon announced an air offensive, code-named Linebacker, against North Vietnam. The principal targets included the classic targets of a strategic air offensive, including seaports, the railroad network, fuel storage facilities, and surface-to-air (SAM) missile sites. Eight years after it was first proposed by Curtis LeMay, North Vietnamese ports would also be mined.

Many technological advances that had occurred since 1968 made the aerial battlefield of Linebacker different from that of Rolling Thunder. On the American side, laser-guided weapons made it possible to hit targets with more precision. On the other side, however, the enemy had now built—thanks to help from the Soviets—an expanded air defense system that was second only to that of the Soviet Union itself. Advanced radar, together with newer SAMs and MiG-21 interceptors made North Vietnam a formidable foe. American pilots faced some of the most intense air-to-air combat of the war. The only American fighter pilots to achieve "ace" status (five or more aerial victories) over Vietnam, did so during Linebacker.

Although the Linebacker operations successfully blunted the North Vietnamese offensive by the early fall of 1972, and tactical air operations wound down, negotiations with North Vietnam aimed at bringing the war to an end were going nowhere.

During Linebacker, as the U.S. Air Force had funneled a large number of tactical aircraft into the theater to augment PACAF assets, SAC undertook a major buildup of its B-52 force. Under Operation Bullet Shot, 161 B-52D and B-52G aircraft were sent out from the United States, thus bringing the total deployment to 210, the highest number of BUFFs that had yet been deployed to Southeast Asia and over half of SAC's total B-52 fleet.

To ready them for the air defense environment they would soon encounter, about half of the B-52Gs deployed overseas were brought up to date with the same electronic countermeasures upgrades with which the Arc Light B-52Ds had been retrofitted between 1967 and 1969.

Under the Phase V ECM Fit, better known as the Rivet Rambler program, these B-52Gs received the AN/ALR-18 automatic radar receiver, the AN/ALR-20 wideband countermeasures receiver, the AN/ALT-16 barrage-jamming system, AN/ALT-32H high-band jammers, AN/ALT-32L low-band jammers, AN/ALT-6B or AN/ALT-22 continuous wave jamming transmitters, and the AN/APR-25 radar homing and warning system. They also were fitted with AN/ALE-20 flare dispensers and AN/ALE-24 chaff dispensers to confuse radar and SAM sensors. The B-52Gs did not, however, have their conventional bomb capacity increased as the B-52Ds had with the Big Belly upgrade back in 1965.

The urgency of the upgrades was underscored on November 22, 1972, when a B-52D was hit by a North Vietnamese SAM for the first time. Damaged during a raid on Vinh, the BUFF went down, although the pilot managed to maneuver it over nonhostile territory, and the crew successfully escaped.

The B-52Gs had yet to make their combat debut, and the fact that not all had received Rivet Rambler upgrades would soon present itself as a serious problem.

Linebacker II

By December, negotiations at the peace talks in Paris had devolved into bickering, accusations, counter-accusations, and disagreements between the United States and its South Vietnamese allies. Finally, on December 16, the North Vietnamese delegation walked out

without setting a date for a resumption of talks. At this juncture, the Nixon administration made the decision to undertake a major strategic air offensive against the industrial and logistical heart of North Vietnam using B-52s. It was essentially the same strategy proposed by Curtis LeMay seven years earlier.

Operation Linebacker II was conceived as a three-night "maximum effort" using B-52s for a strategic air offensive targeting facilities in and around Hanoi and Haiphong, many of which had been off-limits to American aircraft, even during Rolling Thunder. Scheduled to begin on December 18, 1972, this campaign would be sending the BUFFs into a concentrated air defense environment that had claimed its first B-52 just a few weeks before.

On December 18, a total of 129 bombers were launched, beginning with 42 veteran B-52Ds flying from U-Tapao, followed by 87 BUFFs from Andersen AFB on Guam, which included 54 newly arrived B-52Gs. They operated in three-plane cells for mutual ECM protection and were supported by a large fleet of KC-135 tankers and by fighter escorts and tactical ECM aircraft that preceded the bombers into the target area.

The targets for the first night included rail yards and logistical facilities in and around Hanoi, as well as the MiG bases at Kep, Hoa Loc, and Phuc Yen. In retrospect, mission planners should have put more emphasis on SAM sites that first night. The SAMs downed three BUFFs on December 18, but the interceptors claimed none. However, Sgt. Samuel Turner shot down a MiG-21 to become the first B-52 tail gunner to shoot down an enemy aircraft.

Despite the losses, the results of the bombing were deemed good, with the bombs having struck more than 90 percent of the assigned targets.

On December 19, a total of ninety-three BUFFs, making the grueling fourteen-hour round trip from Guam, struck rail yards and a power plant, successfully returning to their bases without a loss. The following night, ninety-nine bombers struck Hanoi in three

■ An "elephant walk" of B-52D Stratofortress aircraft line up on the sway-backed runway at Andersen AFB for takeoff as they prepare for strikes over Hanoi and Haiphong in North Vietnam. *USAF*

■ A view of Strategic Air Command B-52D and B-52G Stratofortresses, crowded on the ramps at Andersen AFB in December 1972 prior to Linebacker II operations over North Vietnam. *USAF*

■ A B-52D Stratofortress waits beside the runway as a B-52G approaches for landing after completing a bombing mission over North Vietnam. *USAF*

■ Trailing smoke from their J57s, B-52Gs take off, one after another, from Andersen AFB for bombing missions over North Vietnam. *USAF*

■ Linebacker II marked the most activity the field at Andersen AFB had seen since it was used by B-29s against Japan in 1945. A B-52G is seen here landing as a B-52D prepares to take off. *USAF*

(cont. from p. 93) waves, as had the bombers on the previous two nights. Unfortunately, mission planners had chosen not to alter the routing scenario, and the North Vietnamese had been able to concentrate their defenses where they knew the bombers would be.

Having used their defenses sparingly on December 19, the enemy turned them on full blast. Over 220 SAMs were launched at the three waves, with aircrews reporting a higher degree of accuracy than on the first two nights. On December 20, SAC lost six B-52s to enemy SAMs, with most being B-52Gs without the improved Rivet Rambler ECM packages. The B-52Gs also proved less capable of absorbing battle damage than the B-52Ds. Their lighter structural weight, which gave them greater range, also contributed to the B-52Gs being more vulnerable to enemy fire.

It stunned the U.S. Air Force to have lost nine of its biggest bombers in just three nights—but there was no turning back.

The Nixon administration decided that the three-night maximum effort would now be an effort of indefinite duration, though for the next four nights, the size of the effort would be cut to just thirty bombers. Except for the night of December 23, when a dozen BUFFs flew in from Andersen, all of these thirty-plane missions would originate from U-Tapao.

With a painful lesson having been learned, mission planners changed the routing for each night's mission, varied the altitude, employed more extensive ECM, and spread radar-jamming chaff more broadly. In addition to rail yards, petroleum storage, and other logistical facilities, the target lists now included SAM sites.

The only losses during those four nights were two that occurred on December 21. On both December 22 and 23, the bombers feinted toward one target before making a sudden turn toward another. The missions of December 22–24 were against unpredictable targets, so the enemy had lost the ability to lie in wait with their most potent defenses.

The mission of December 24, Christmas Eve, repeated the scenario of the previous two. Once again, thirty BUFFs, this time all from U-Tapao, went out, struck rail yards at Thai Nguyen and Kep, 40 miles north and northeast of Hanoi, and returned unharmed. Two of the cells were attacked unsuccessfully by MiGs, with one MiG-21 shot down by Airman First Class Albert Moore, the second B-52 tail gunner to get a confirmed MiG kill during the Vietnam War.

On Christmas Day, the entire B-52 force paused for a twenty-four-hour halt in what the world press was now calling "the Christmas bombings." The Nixon administration also suggested that the stand-down would be an opportunity for the North Vietnamese to reconsider their intransigence at the Paris peace conference.

Sgt. Samuel Turner, a B-52D tail gunner, was awarded the Silver Star for shooting down a MiG-21 on December 18, 1972, near Hanoi. It was one of only two enemy aircraft ever downed by a BUFF gunner. *USAF*

They didn't.

Linebacker II resumed on December 26 with another maximum effort involving 120 BUFFs, 78 of which took off from Andersen. They attacked in ten waves, hitting Haiphong, and seven separate target complexes in Hanoi. Unlike the earlier hundred plane raids, which were spread out over several hours, the entire December 26 force hit their targets in the space of fifteen minutes, pushing enemy defenses to the limit. The strike package was preceded by tactical aircraft attacking SAM and antiaircraft artillery batteries.

Of 113 bombers who arrived over the target, only 2 were lost to SAMs. The absence of the SAM missile batteries that had been taken out by B-52s on the December 23 raids saved lives on December 26. Meanwhile, ECM had also been refined by teams working around the clock since the first missions. Indeed, no aircraft were lost from a three-plane cell using mutual ECM protection. The two that were lost had been from cells whose third member had been forced to turn back prior to arriving over the target.

For the next three nights, the maximum effort was stepped down to sixty BUFFs each night, half of which flew out of U-Tapao and half from Andersen. Mission planners called for all sixty of the bombers to release their bombs in a ten-minute time span.

The attack on the night of December 27 targeted supply dumps, rail yards, and SAM batteries on the north and south sides of Hanoi. Also struck was Lang Dang, the principal choke point on the main rail line leading in from China, which made it a key

A B-52D Stratofortress is silhouetted against the sun, as it flies over the cloud-covered Pacific Ocean. *USAF*

strategic objective. The two BUFFs lost that night to SAMs were the last B-52s lost to enemy fire during the war.

By the following night, the B-52 operations were becoming routine, even as the damage on the ground mounted. In the beginning, the North Vietnamese were launching around two hundred SAMs nightly, usually in salvos. On December 29, they were able to launch just twenty-three.

The last bomb of Linebacker II fell at seventeen minutes before midnight on December 29, 1972, bringing to a close the most intensive strategic air offensive since World War II. In 729 missions, the B-52s had dropped 15,000 tons of bombs and had dodged more than 1,200 SAMs. There had been fifteen BUFFs shot down, eight crewmen killed, thirty-three captured and later repatriated, and twenty-five missing in action.

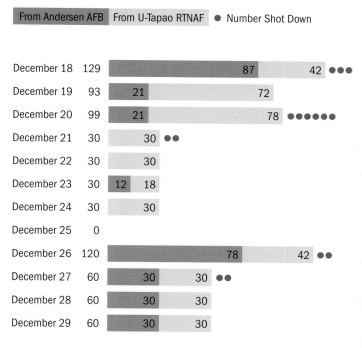

Linebacker II: Sorties Day By Day

From Andersen AFB   From U-Tapao RTNAF   ● Number Shot Down

Date	Total	Andersen	U-Tapao	Shot Down
December 18	129	87	42	●●●
December 19	93	21	72	
December 20	99	21	78	●●●●●●
December 21	30		30	●●
December 22	30		30	
December 23	30	12	18	
December 24	30		30	
December 25	0			
December 26	120	78	42	●●
December 27	60	30	30	●●
December 28	60	30	30	
December 29	60	30	30	

In their wake, the bombers left nearly all of North Vietnam's electricity generating capacity in shambles and a quarter of its petroleum reserves destroyed. Rail lines had been cut in five hundred places, with several hundred locomotives and railcars put out of business. Though Hanoi and Haiphong felt the brunt of Linebacker II, perhaps the most telling effect was felt half a world away at the Paris peace talks, which resumed on January 8, 1973, with an agreement signed finally on January 27.

Although in the shadow of an operation like Linebacker II almost any other operation is anticlimactic, the Arc Light missions did continue. The last B-52 missions against both South Vietnam and North Vietnam (south of the 20th parallel) were flown on same day that the Paris peace accords were signed. The last B-52 missions over Laos were flown in mid-April. The BUFFs continued to fly missions over Cambodia against the rebel forces advancing on Phnom Penh until they were halted by the congressional ban on bombing. The last B-52 sortie in Southeast Asia was flown there on August 15.

If Linebacker II had not ended the war, it *had* proved once again that strategic air power had the potential to be the decisive factor in the defeat of an enemy. The B-52, meanwhile, proved to be one of the war's most important weapons. When used to project strategic air power, BUFFs drove the North Vietnamese to seek a ceasefire and sufficiently throttled their war-making capabilities so that they were unable to launch another major offensive for more than two years.

THE 1970S WOULD BE a decade of consolidation, as most Stratofortress variants were retired and remaining variants upgraded. For eight years, the SAC B-52 fleet had operated with one foot in the world of conventional bombing operations, while still maintaining its nuclear deterrent mission. Ironically, those same years saw a dramatic decrease in the overall size of the fleet. In December 1965, even as the B-52Ds were being improved for the start of their role in the Southeast Asia conflict, Robert McNamara announced a long-term Stratofortress phaseout program.

His plan was that most Stratofortresses would be sent to join the entire B-58 fleet in long-term storage at the boneyard of the Military Aircraft Storage and Disposition Center (MASDC) at Davis-Monthan AFB in Arizona. Though the process was slowed during the war, it nevertheless continued.

SAC had maintained a fleet of around 600 Stratofortresses through the first half of the 1960s, but thereafter, a rapid rate of retirements brought the total to 505 in 1969, and 402 by the time of Linebacker II in 1972. With a few exceptions, the B-52Bs were out of service by 1966, followed by most B-52Cs and B-52Es by 1971. Some high-time war-veteran B-52Fs were retired by 1968, though the last few B-52Fs were not gone until the end of 1978.

Meanwhile, the two longer-range, second-generation aircraft, the B-52G and B-52H, would be retained. So too would the B-52D, in which so many improvements had been made to optimize it for conventional weapons delivery. As noted in the previous chapter, the upgrades made during Arc Light had actually made the B-52D more capable than the B-52G with regard to electronic countermeasures.

By 1978, thirty-seven high-time B-52Ds were retired and sent to MASDC, but eighty B-52Ds were earmarked for extensive modifications under the Pacer Plank program. Undertaken by Boeing, Pacer Plank included partial reskinning of the wings and fuselage, as well as wing pylon modification. As William Holder points out in the July-August 1978 issue of the *Air University Review*, "a surprising phenomenon resulted from the Pacer Plank modifications. The new wing skin is much cleaner aerodynamically than the skin it replaced, resulting in considerably less drag. Even though the modified plane weighs about 3,400 pounds more, its cruise range has been increased by three percent."

The Pacer Plank B-52Ds remained active until being retired in 1982–1983.

Meanwhile, the B-52G and B-52H were also in need of improving. The Linebacker II experience, in which six B-52Gs were lost to North Vietnamese SAMs, pointed out serious shortcomings in the aircraft that was intended to penetrate Soviet air defenses

B-52s in the SAC Inventory:
Draw-down and Early-Model Retirement Era

Numbers exclude aircraft not assigned to SAC

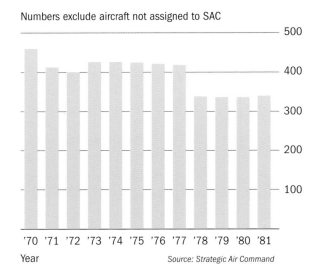

'70 '71 '72 '73 '74 '75 '76 '77 '78 '79 '80 '81

Year   Source: Strategic Air Command

if the Cold War turned hot. With this in mind, the B-52G and B-52H aircraft were the subject of numerous upgrades during the 1970s, including the Phase VI ECM Defensive Avionics Systems retrofit, better known as the Rivet Ace program.

Undertaken between 1971 and 1976, the Phase VI Rivet Ace bore some similarity to the Phase V Rivet Rambler program of the late 1960s, as they both included the AN/ALT-32H high-band and AN/ALT-32L low-band jammers, and the AN/ALR-20A wideband countermeasures receiver. They both included the AN/ALT-16 barrage jamming transmitters, though the Rivet Ace AN/ALT-16A was driven by the AN/ALQ-122 false target generator system.

Both upgrades included retrofitting eight AN/ALE-24 chaff dispensers, with a total of 1,125 bundles of chaff, but while Rivet Rambler incorporated six AN/ALE-20 flare dispensers, the Linebacker II experienced dictated double that number under Rivet Ace. Other important components of Rivet Ace included the AN/ALQ-117 active countermeasures system, AN/ALQ-153 tail-warning radar, and the AN/ALT-28 jamming transmitter.

The package also included the Litton AN/ALR-46 digital radar warning receiver, AN/ALQ-117 active countermeasures, and the AN/ALQ-153 tail warning radar.

Among the most noticeable upgrades was the installation of the AN/ASQ-151 Electro-optical Viewing System (EVS) to give crews improved visibility at low level during nocturnal operations. The EVS included a Westinghouse AN/AVQ-22 Low-Light-level Television (LLTV) camera, and a Hughes AN/AAQ-6 Forward-Looking Infrared (FLIR) sensor, both located in conspicuous fairings on the underside of the forward fuselage.

Meanwhile, the parallel Quick Start program of 1974 retrofitted the B-52Gs and B-52Hs with cartridge starters, which permitted a simultaneous ignition of all eight engines.

By 1976, the B-52Gs and B-52Hs had been upgraded with the Phase VI ECM Defensive Avionics Systems package, as well as the AN/ASQ-151 Electro-optical Viewing System. Beginning in 1980, the Stratofortress's offensive avionics were replaced by newer equipment. The ancient analog AN/ASQ-38 bombing-navigation system was superseded by the AN/ASQ-176 Offensive Avionics System (OAS), which had solid-state digital electronics. This package included the AN/ASN-134 attitude heading reference system, the AN/ASN-136 inertial navigation system, AN/APN-218 Doppler radar, and the AN/APN-224 radar altimeter.

A Phase VI–Plus ECM upgrade followed in 1988, which involved the AN/ALQ-117 Pave Mint active countermeasures system being replaced by the improved AN/ALQ-172(V)1 in the B-52G and the AN/ALQ-172(V)2 in the B-52H.

The Postwar Role of the Stratofortress

By the late 1960s, the Stratofortress was an established component of a three-part nuclear deterrent force that was known as the Strategic Triad. The other prongs of the Triad were both solid-fueled missiles with intercontinental range: Intercontinental Ballistic Missiles (ICBMs), also under the command and control of the Strategic Air Command; and Submarine-Launched Ballistic Missiles (SLBMs), controlled by the U.S. Navy. The two missile types were deployed throughout the decade, superseding an earlier generation of inefficient liquid-fueled ICBMs. By the early 1970s, SAC was deploying its multiple-warhead LGM-30G Minuteman III, and the U.S. Navy, its long-lived UGM-73 Poseidon.

The Triad, despite involving strike forces of two separate branches of the armed services, operated under a Single Integrated Operational Plan (SIOP). This frequently updated document assigned priorities to target lists and specified detailed mission plans for each leg of the Triad. Revised annually, the SIOP originated in 1962, superseding the

A SAC B-52D Stratofortress overflies the Soviet aircraft carrier *Kiev* while on a routine maritime reconnaissance mission over international waters. *USAF*

Stratofortresses undergoing routine maintenance in November 1977 at the Oklahoma Air Logistics Center at Tinker AFB. *USAF photo, Sgt. Deal Toney*

The BUFF pilot "paints" a picture of California's Mount Shasta (visible in the distance) using his aircraft's AN/ASQ-151 Electro-optical Viewing System. Unnecessary in broad daylight, the capability was very useful during low-level operations at night. This system was state of the art in 1980. *Bill Yenne*

The view from the right seat of a 328th Bombardment Squadron B-52H as photographed by the author during a low-level training mission over the First Combat Evaluation Group Detachment 5 range near Wilder, Idaho, on June 25, 1980. *Bill Yenne*

National Strategic Target List (NSTL), which had originated at the White House level in 1960. The SIOP continued to be updated past the end of the Cold War, being replaced by the Operational Plan (OPLAN) in 2003, which has since reportedly been superseded by the multiple Contingency Plans (CONPLAN).

Each successive SIOP was drafted against the backdrop of increasing Soviet nuclear capability. In the mid-1960s, the United States had a four-to-one lead over the Soviet Union in ICBMs, but the ratio inverted to favor the Soviets three-to-two in both ICBMs and SLBMs during the 1970s, with new weapons being developed and produced at a rapid rate. The United States still had a three-to-one lead over the Soviets in strategic bombers, but that was primarily the dwindling B-52 fleet. The mainstay of the Soviet fleet was still the Tupolev Tu-95, codenamed Bear by NATO, which is seen by many as having originated as a knockoff of the turboprop Boeing Model 464-35.

The Ongoing Quest For a Successor

During the early days of the SIOP, Secretary of Defense McNamara had made no secret of his fondness for a reliance on missiles, rather than manned bombers, and so he put a low priority on this point of the triad.

The Achilles heel of the manned bomber, as McNamara pointed out, was the growing capability of Soviet air defenses. Designed as a high-altitude bomber, the B-52 had to compromise and be adapted to fly at low level to penetrate these defenses. As for air defenses, the specter of the six BUFFs lost during a single night during Linebacker II still haunted strategic planners despite post-Vietnam Rivet Ace upgrades in B-52 ECM capabilities.

By the 1970s, the sprawling Soviet air defense network was far more sophisticated than that which SAC crews had faced in Linebacker II. It included 6,000 radar installations from Murmansk to Vladivostok and 12,000 SAMs in around a thousand locations. Meanwhile, the Soviet interceptor force was estimated to include 5,000 aircraft, including the Mach 3 MiG-25 Foxbat, which entered service in 1970, and which had "look-down/shoot-down" radar to permit attacks on low-flying B-52s.

■ The copilot's station in a retired B-52D. Note that the "hood ornament" in the center of the yoke, highly valued by collectors, has been removed. *Bill Yenne*

■ The North American Aviation XB-70 Valkyrie was intended by the SAC to be the prototype for the successor to the Stratofortress in the 1960s, but was canceled by President John F. Kennedy as "unnecessary and economically unjustifiable." *USAF*

■ Left: Harold Brown, called "the Father of the B-1" for his advocacy of the Advanced Manned Strategic Aircraft program while chief of research and engineering at the Pentagon in the Johnson administration, was instrumental in killing the B-1 program while Secretary of Defense in the Carter administration. *DoD* ■ Right: The SAC insignia was prominent on the nose of the first Rockwell B-1 when it rolled out from Air Force Plant 42 at Palmdale, California, on October 26, 1974.

The second B-1A aircraft was reconfigured to serve as the testbed for the B-1B Test Program at the Air Force Flight Test Center at Edwards AFB in 1983. *USAF photo, Samuel Hotton*

In September 1987, during the author's visit to Palmdale, the B-1B *Spirit of Abilene* was being finished up for its final delivery flight to SAC's 7th Bombardment Wing at Dyess AFB near Abilene, Texas. *Bill Yenne*

As for a new generation of bombers, it had been assumed when the YB-52 first flew that the entire Stratofortress fleet would have been superseded by another aircraft type well before the 1970s. The B-52 had began replacing the B-36 in SAC service by 1956, only eight years after the B-36 had first entered service, but McNamara consistently rejected serious discussion of a new intercontinental-range jet bomber. By the middle of the 1960s, the supersonic B-58 was phased out, and the XB-70 program was cancelled without going beyond the two prototypes.

The issue of a successor to the B-52 had been a persistent topic of conversation from the industry design rooms to the Pentagon throughout the 1960s as the B-58 and XB-70 came and went—and as McNamara limited the Advanced Manned Strategic Aircraft

Dozens of Stratofortresses, including many B-52Cs, in long-term storage at the Military Aircraft Storage and Disposition Center (MASDC) at Davis-Monthan AFB in Arizona, May 1971. *USAF*

(AMSA) program to a series of lengthy studies. In 1969, SAC began receiving the first of more than sixty General Dynamics FB-111 aircraft, a longer-winged variant of the F-111 fighter, but these aircraft were seen as an "interim" bomber and never as a successor to the B-52.

In 1969, the incoming Nixon administration revived the AMSA program with the goal of evolving it into a real strategic bomber. A design by North American Rockwell was chosen over those submitted by Boeing and General Dynamics, and the designation B-1A was assigned. The design of this supersonic bomber included a variable geometry "swing" wing, such as had been used on the F-111 family of fighters and the Grumman F-14 Tomcat fighter, to provide high lift during takeoff and landing, and low drag during the high speeds necessary in combat.

A total of 244 B-1As, including 4 flight-test aircraft, were planned, with the first to enter SAC service by 1979, but the former number was revised downward, as the date was pushed out. The first B-1A flight occurred in December 1974, and an extensive flight test program got underway against the backdrop of growing debate over whether a manned strategic bomber could ever successfully get through Soviet air defenses.

In turn, the B-1A became a contentious issue in the 1976 presidential election campaign. President Gerald Ford favored the B-1A for its performance and its flexibility, while his challenger, Georgia Governor Jimmy Carter, told the Democratic Platform Committee that the bomber was "an example of a proposed system which should not be funded and would be wasteful of taxpayers' dollars" and promised to kill the program if he was elected.

As *Time* magazine reported, "Both sides in the debate agree that the B-l is the hottest bomber ever flown. But is it worth its $102 million price tag? Can it reach targets deep within the Soviet Union if there is a nuclear war? These questions are especially important because, according to present strategy, close to 60 percent of the U.S.

The B-52D Stratofortress named *Diamond Lil,* covered in snow at the USAF Academy in Colorado Springs. This display aircraft welcomes visitors to the academy. *USAF photo, Mike Kaplan*

A B-52D is scrapped in accordance with the SALT II. The nose sections of the other two B-52 carcasses are lying on the ground below. *USAF photo, Sgt. Daniel Perez*

■ AGM-69 SRAMs and Mk 28 thermonuclear bombs (background) in the bomb bay of a B-52H at Ellsworth AFB during Exercise Global Shield in April 1984. *USAF photo, Sgt. Boyd Belcher*

■ Crews from the 92nd Bombardment Wing load AGM-86B ALCMs aboard a B-52G during the November 1985 SAC Combat Weapons Loading Competition at Ellsworth AFB. *USAF photo, Sgt. Rose Reynolds*

■ Airmen load an ATM-84A, the training variant of the AGM-84A Harpoon missile, onto the wing of a B-52G in November 1988. *USAF photo, Chief Master Sgt. Don Sutherland*

nuclear megatonnage will be carried by manned bombers, the rest by missiles based on land and aboard submarines. Concedes Democratic Senator Sam Nunn, a B-1 backer: 'Considerable logic can be mustered for either side of the argument.'"

When Carter *was* elected, he appointed as his Secretary of Defense the same man who had helped kill the XB-70 and initiate AMSA—Harold Brown. In January 1977, Brown told reporters that "the big advantage [of a manned bomber such as the B-52 or the B-1A] is that it complicates the other side's problems. The question is how much can you afford to pay for that as compared to the other ways you could spend the funds."

When reminded of his earlier role in AMSA, and that he had been called the "Father of the B-1," Brown went on to say: "Yes, I started the so-called Advanced Manned Strategic Aircraft Program. But it's a long way from studies to hardware, and I won't take credit or blame for the full gestation and early childhood of that particular offspring."

Finally, on June 30, 1977, Carter and Brown let the axe fall, announcing that the B-1A program, beyond flight testing the first four aircraft, would be terminated. The announcement came just forty-eight hours after the House of Representatives had rejected an amendment to delete the program from the defense budget. Robert Lindsey, writing in the *New York Times* business section, said that the news hit the forty thousand executives, technicians and assembly-line workers assigned to the B-1A program "like a shell burst."

Congressman Robert Dornan of California, where the B-1A would have been built, commented that "they're breaking out the vodka and caviar in Moscow."

They may well have been toasting the B-1A cancellation, but they certainly would not be toasting the system that was to come next.

Even as a manned bomber to replace the B-52 was no longer in the works, the Defense Department was about to move forward with another plan. This was to arm the B-52G and B-52H with a new weapon that was being called the cruise missile.

Of this weapon, the Soviet news agency Tass complained, "The implementation of these militaristic plans has seriously complicated efforts for the limitation of the strategic arms race."

Stand-Off Missiles, the Second Generation

The term *cruise missile*, which was mentioned so widely in the media during the late 1970s as the "next big thing" in strategic offense, was actually applicable to several weapons, but for SAC, it meant the Boeing AGM-86 Air-Launched Cruise Missile (ALCM). Though the ALCM earned the headlines, it was one of two air-launched strategic missiles developed and deployed primarily to enhance the B-52 in the late Cold War period.

The first was the Boeing AGM-69 Short-Range Attack Missile (SRAM). It was originally conceived in 1964 as a successor to the AGM-28 Hound Dog. With a length of 15 feet 10 inches, and a weight of 2,230 pounds, the SRAM was one-third the size of a Hound Dog, but a Stratofortress could carry many more of them. Operationally, B-52s could mount eight AGM-69As internally on a rotary launcher, as well as a dozen externally—compared with just two Hound Dogs on the underwing pylons. The FB-111, meanwhile, could carry six. An AGM-69B (SRAM B) was developed for the B-1A, but this weapon was cancelled when the B-1A program was terminated.

As the name implies, the range was short—only about 100 miles compared with 700 for the Hound Dog. Both missiles used inertial guidance, but the Hound Dog was powered by a Pratt & Whitney J52 turbojet while the SRAM had a Lockheed SR75 two-stage solid-fuel rocket. The SRAM was armed with a W69 thermonuclear warhead, derived from the B61 bomb, and had a yield of up to 200 kilotons.

The first AGM-69A test flight came in July 1969, and the AGM-69A SRAM entered service aboard SAC B-52s in 1972. Boeing built around 1,500 through 1975. Having reached a peak number of 1,451 in 1975, there were still more than a thousand in the Strategic Air Command inventory in 1990 when they were withdrawn from service.

The ALCM, meanwhile, was clearly a generation ahead of the SRAM. It had a range of 1,500 miles, twice that of the Hound Dog, therefore making it a significant improvement in terms of stand-off capability. Being 20 feet 9 inches long and weighing 3,200 pounds, the operational ALCM is only slightly larger than the SRAM, and much smaller than a Hound Dog.

Boeing designed the AGM-86 so that its air intake, wings, elevons, and vertical tail surfaces are all folded into the fuselage until they are deployed. The compact profile of the folded ALCM made possible the development of an eight-missile rotary launcher that was installed in the bomb bays of 82 B-52Hs. Meanwhile, all ninety-six existing B-52Hs and ninety-eight B-52Gs were equipped to carry six ALCMs on each of two underwing pylons.

Under the terms of the SALT II agreement of 1979, the ALCM-armed B-52Gs were modified with a distinctive wing root fairing called a "strakelet" so that they could be identified and monitored by Soviet reconnaissance satellites. The B-52Hs were not marked with strakelets as it was common knowledge that *all* of them were modified to carry ALCMs.

Those B-52Gs not armed with ALCMs were retrofitted with Heavy Stores Adapter Beams (HSAB) in place of the older underwing pylons. Like the upgrades to the B-52D

A pair of F-4E Phantom IIs fly in formation with a 2nd Bombardment Wing B-52G during the 15th Air Force's first "shootout" bombing competition in May 1989. *USAF photo, Sgt. Michael Haggerty*

that had been carried out two decades earlier, the HSAB provided the capability of carrying a much greater conventional weapons load, including Mk 55 bottom mines or Mk 56 moored mines.

Whereas the Hound Dog utilized turbojet power, and the SRAM was rocket-propelled, the ALCM was equipped with a Williams F107-WR-100 turbofan engine. The operational AGM-86Bs were armed with W80 thermonuclear warheads with a yield up to 170 kilotons. Developed from the B61 thermonuclear bomb, the W80 was also used in the General Dynamics BGM-109 Tomahawk cruise missile.

The principal feature that made the ALCM a revolutionary weapons system was its low-level flight characteristics. One of the major technological breakthroughs of the 1970s was Terrain Contour Matching (TERCOM), which was combined with early Global Positioning System (GPS) capability in a guidance system that would allow a cruise missile to navigate autonomously in three dimensions at low level.

The AGM-86B entered production in 1980 and became operational in December 1982 with SAC's 416th Bombardment Wing at Griffiss AFB in New York. The production of a total of 1,715 missiles was completed in October 1986.

In the meantime, the U.S. Air Force decided on a conventional future for part of its ALCM inventory. In June 1986 a small number of AGM-86B missiles were converted to conventional weapons. Their nuclear warheads were replaced by a high-explosive blast fragmentation warhead, and they were redesignated as the AGM-86C Conventional Air-Launched Cruise Missile (CALCM).

This modification also replaced the AGM-86B's TERCOM guidance system with an internal GPS capability within the existing inertial navigation computer system. Beginning in 1996, additional ALCMs were converted as AGM-86C CALCMs as well as to AGM-86D Block II CALCMs, which were like the AGM-86C but armed with a hardened target penetrating warhead. Both CALCMs were designed to be air-launched by B-52Hs, either from the rotary launcher or underwing pylon.

While the AGM-86 family has been the signature strategic stand-off armament of the Stratofortress since the 1980s, the B-52G's HSAB permitted it to carry six McDonnell

■ An air-to-air front view of a 416th Bombardment Wing B-52G armed with AGM-86B Air-Launched Cruise Missiles (ALCMs). *USAF*

■ An air-to-air view of a KC-10A Extender refueling a B-52G Stratofortress in February 1981. *USAF*

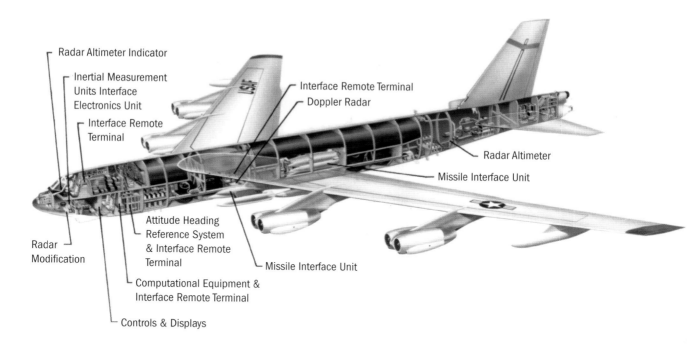

Radar Altimeter Indicator

Inertial Measurement Units Interface Electronics Unit

Interface Remote Terminal

Interface Remote Terminal

Doppler Radar

Radar Altimeter

Missile Interface Unit

Radar Modification

Attitude Heading Reference System & Interface Remote Terminal

Missile Interface Unit

Computational Equipment & Interface Remote Terminal

Controls & Displays

Douglas (Boeing after 1997) AGM-84 Harpoon antiship missiles. The Harpoon is the air-launched variant of a widely deployed family of antiship missiles that includes the ship-launched RGM-84 and submarine-launched UGM-84 first deployed with the U.S. Navy in 1977.

Around thirty B-52Gs were tasked with maritime patrols, armed with Harpoons, and fitted with a Harpoon Aircraft Command Launch Control Set (HACLCS). Beginning in 1984, they were assigned to Loring AFB in Maine and Andersen AFB on Guam.

A cutaway illustration showing areas singled out for B-52G electronics systems upgrades. *USAF*

The Cold War, the Final Decade

Throughout the 1970s, as SAC was drawing down its B-52 force and various entities throughout the United States government were debating a potential replacement, there was an ongoing diplomatic effort aimed at a draw-down of global nuclear weapons capability. The United States and the Soviet Union had reached the point where, to paraphrase Robert McNamara's MAD doctrine, the mutual destruction of the two powers was assured.

Earlier efforts to cool the growth and proliferation of nuclear stockpiles had resulted in the 1963 Partial Nuclear Test Ban Treaty and the 1968 Nuclear Non-Proliferation Treaty. It also led to the beginning of an ongoing dialogue, the Strategic Arms Limitation Talks (SALT).

The first fruit of these bilateral talks was the 1972 Anti-Ballistic Missile Treaty, as well as an agreement to freeze the number of strategic ballistic missile launchers

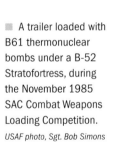
An air-to-air left rear view of a B-52G as it flies over the Egyptian pyramids at Giza, 12 miles southwest of central Cairo, during exercise Bright Star '83. *USAF*

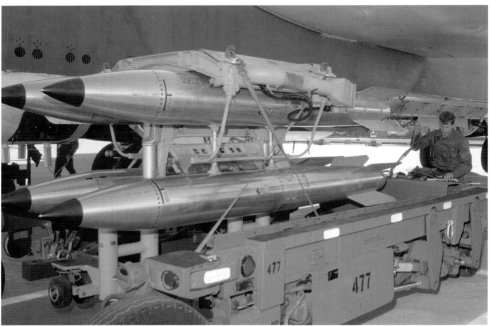

A trailer loaded with B61 thermonuclear bombs under a B-52 Stratofortress, during the November 1985 SAC Combat Weapons Loading Competition.
USAF photo, Sgt. Bob Simons

at existing levels. This meant that new SLBM and ICBM launchers were acceptable so long as an equal number of older launchers were taken off-line. For SAC, the Minuteman III deployment was already at its intended level, and reducing the number of B-52s beyond the number retired by the McNamara draw-down opened the door to the deployment of another strategic bomber such as the B-1A, which was in development during the 1970s.

A second round of SALT talks aimed at ending the manufacture of nuclear weapons and reducing the number of launchers led to the SALT II agreement, which was signed by Soviet leader Leonid Brezhnev and President Jimmy Carter in Vienna on June 18, 1979.

However, as the United States was reducing its fleet, the Soviets were not. At the same time that SAC was decommissioning B-52s and Carter was canceling the B-1A, the Soviet Union had gone forward with its equivalent of the B-1A, the supersonic Tupolev Tu-22, code-named Backfire by NATO. The Soviets were also building a new class of ICBMs, the SS-17 through SS-19, which had Multiple Independently targetable Reentry Vehicle (MIRV) capability of ten or more warheads each, while the Minuteman III had just three.

President Ronald Reagan took office in January 1981 as the Soviet Union was rapidly expanding its global offensive capacity and pushing new weapons through every loophole in the SALT II treaty.

In the foreword to the 1981 Defense Department publication *Soviet Military Power*, Reagan's defense secretary, Caspar Weinberger, wrote that "we have witnessed the continuing growth of Soviet military power at a pace that shows no signs of slackening in the future." He went on to say that "There is nothing hypothetical about the Soviet military

A B-52 Stratofortress from the 416th Bombardment Wing prepares to land at Elmendorf AFB in Alaska during Amalgam Warrior 1988. *USAF photo, Master Sgt. Ed Boyce*

machine. Its expansion, modernization, and contribution to projection of power beyond Soviet boundaries are obvious."

Reagan's approach to the Soviet build up was different than that of his predecessors. Though he sought the same goal of a world free of the nuclear threat, he realized that it could only be achieved from a position of strength rather than a position of weakness. His perspective on weapons development was vigorously expansive, with emphasis on both defensive and offensive hardware. Announced in March 1983, his view of nuclear defense was the Strategic Defense Initiative, a wide range of research programs aimed at studying the feasibility of defending against ICBMs.

At the same time, he undertook the largest upgrade and modernization of the American armed forces in nearly three decades. This included a broad program of cruise missile development, which included not only the ALCM for the U.S. Air Force, but the Tomahawk Land Attack Missile (TLAM) for the U.S. Navy and the similar Ground-Launched Cruise Missile (GLCM) for the U.S. Air Force. For the Strategic Air Command, it also meant moving forward on the ten-warhead LGM-118 Peacekeeper ICBM, as well as a revival of the B-1 program, the super-secret program that led to the B-2, and modernization of the B-52 fleet.

The B-1 was revived under a Reagan administration initiative known as the Long-Range Combat Aircraft (LRCA), which sought a strategic bomber that could augment the Stratofortresses in SAC inventory. The obvious answer was an updated variation on the B-1A. Rockwell got the green light, and Reagan announced in October 1981 that one hundred of such aircraft would be acquired under the designation B-1B. Using two existing B-1As as testbeds, the aircraft was redesigned with a reduced radar

Trading reflective white undersides for camouflage gray: a July 1984 view of a newly repainted 92nd Bombardment Wing B-52G at Fairchild AFB.

USAF photo, Sgt. Bob Simons

cross section and other adaptations for both nuclear and conventional bombing missions that took into account the Soviet air defenses of the 1980s. Flight testing of the modified B-1As began in March 1983, and the first production B-1B made its first flight in October 1984. The one hundredth and last B-1B was delivered in May 1988.

The B-2 originated in 1979 under the innocuous-sounding Advanced Technology Bomber (ATB) program. The "advanced technology" was, of course "stealth technology," which was actually a basket of technologies with the goal of reducing the radar cross section of an aircraft to almost nil. In October 1981, even as the contract was let for the B-1A, Northrop Grumman received the contract to build the ATB under the designation B-2A. The huge flying wing, incorporating a myriad of innovations, made its debut flight in July 1989. Originally, the U.S. Air Force intended to acquire 132 B-1Bs, but the aircraft was still on the assembly line when the Cold War ended, and the number was cut to a mere 21.

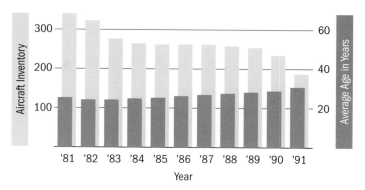

B-52s in the U.S. Air Force Inventory
Reagan Era Through the End of the Cold War

Note: The 1982–1983 period marked the retirement of the B-52D fleet. (The average age goes down as the oldest aircraft are retired.)

Source: Air Force Almanac

These two new strategic bomber programs were understood to complement, rather than to replace, the B-52, though there was clearly an interest in an eventual replacement for a combat aircraft that had already been in front line service longer than any other.

The Stratofortress had survived in service to see the end of nearly half a century of Cold War. If it had been Winston Churchill's 1946 Iron Curtain speech that articulated the fact of the conditions that began the Cold War, it was a speech by Ronald Reagan on June 12, 1987, that marked the beginning of the end. Standing in Berlin, the city blockaded by Josef Stalin in 1948 and divided by the Berlin Wall in 1961, Reagan looked at the Wall, pregnant with symbolism, and issued an invitation to his Soviet counterpart, remarking "General Secretary Gorbachev, if you seek peace, if you seek prosperity for the Soviet Union and Eastern Europe, if you seek liberalization: Come here to this gate! Mr. Gorbachev, open this gate! *Mr. Gorbachev, tear down this Wall!*"

A little more than two years after Ronald Reagan had called for Gorbachev to tear it down, the Berlin Wall *did* come down. It was torn down, however, not by Gorbachev, nor by force of arms, but by the people whom it had imprisoned for more than a generation.

When the Berlin Wall came down in 1989, and the Soviet Union gradually unravelled through the end of 1991, the world breathed a sigh of relief. Having hung over the heads of the world's population for four decades, the Cold War was over.

However, the world was still filled with bellicose dictators, and sinister new threats were even then crawling from their dank, dark holes in Southwest Asia.

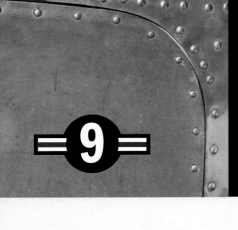

=9= A Storm in the Desert

THE EARLY YEARS of the twentieth century's final decade were marked by major changes in the world, and in the U.S. Air Force deployment of the Stratofortress. Even as the Soviet Union disintegrated, and the Cold War came to an end, the United States fought the Gulf War, its most successful major campaign since World War II—and the Stratofortress was back in sustained combat operations for the first time in two decades.

On October 2, 1990, Iraq's dictator, Saddam Hussein, ordered his army to invade and occupy the oil-rich neighboring state of Kuwait. During Iraq's war with Iran, which had consumed most of the previous decade, Hussein had become deeply indebted to Kuwait and other countries and decided that Kuwait's oil wealth was needed to stave off bankruptcy. Hussein used the tenuous claim that Kuwait *should have been* part of the modern state of Iraq when it was created in 1932 as a pretext for his annexation.

The international community reacted with a United Nations resolution ordering Iraq to withdraw and with a massive military buildup by a broad coalition of world powers aimed initially at preventing an Iraqi invasion of Saudi Arabia and secondarily at ejecting Iraqi forces from Kuwait.

The United States part of this buildup, designated as Operation Desert Shield, saw the deployment of massive quantities of military hardware that had been developed during the Cold War to blunt a Soviet invasion of Western Europe.

The U.S. Air Force role involved the deployment of mainly tactical air power, specifically fighters for air defense and strike aircraft for potential operations against the possible invasion of Saudi Arabia. The Strategic Air Command contribution was in the deployment of tanker aircraft to refuel Coalition aircraft.

Simultaneous with Desert Shield, the Coalition forces prepared for the operation to liberate Kuwait. For the United States, which played the predominant role, this would be known as Operation Desert Storm. The opening phase would involve a massive tactical campaign against Iraqis in Kuwait, as well as a strategic air campaign against Iraq itself.

The overall Coalition commander for Desert Storm was General Norman Schwarzkopf of the U.S. Army—also commander of the United States Central Command (CENTCOM)—with the air campaign, called Operation Instant Thunder, under the command of U.S. Air Force Lieutenant General Chuck Horner, commander of United States Central Command Air Forces (CENTAF).

On August 9, the chairman of the Joint Chiefs of Staff, Gen. Colin Powell, ordered that Stratofortresses also be deployed for possible action. By August 13, B-52Gs from

■ Ordnancemen use an MJ-1 bomb loader to upload M117 750-pound bombs on a BUFF during Operation Desert Shield. *USAF*

the 62nd Bombardment Wing at Carswell AFB and the 69th Bombardment Squadron at Loring AFB, among others, had been deployed to the island of Diego Garcia, a British territory in the Indian Ocean, 3,000 miles south of Kuwait. On August 24, SAC Headquarters issued Special Order GB-084, transferring operational control of its assigned B-52Gs and KC-135s to Horner's CENTAF.

The B-52G was the dedicated Stratofortress type that was to be used in the Gulf War. Diego Garcia would be a key forward operating location, with the bombers operated by the 4300th Provisional Bombardment Wing, but others were added as the operation progressed.

Over the next several months, the B-52Gs flew a number of training sorties over Saudi Arabia, as well as over the Indian Ocean. The intended armament included

Cluster Bombardment Units (CBU), as well as M117 general-purpose 750-pound high-explosive bombs.

The Desert Storm air offensive began on the night of January 16–17, 1991, with the initial targets being Iraqi radar and air defenses, followed by Command, Control, and Communications (C3) facilities. During the first twenty-four hours 2,775 sorties were flown by Coalition strike aircraft.

As part of this effort, the first Stratofortress mission of the Gulf War began on the afternoon of January 16, when seven B-52Gs took off from Barksdale AFB in Louisiana on a marathon thrity-five-hour, nonstop, 14,000-mile round-trip flight. At the time, it was the longest strike mission in the history of aerial warfare. It was the type of capability that had been purposely demonstrated by B-52s in Operation Power Flite three decades earlier.

According to the Department of Defense *Final Report to Congress: Conduct of the Persian Gulf War*, the aircraft launched thirty-five AGM-86C CALCM cruise missiles against "military communications sites and power generation and transmission facilities" in southern Iraq. The CALCM had only just been declared operational earlier in January 1991.

Overshadowed by the milestone mission from Barksdale is the fact that fifteen bombers from the 4300th Provisional Bombardment Wing also struck Iraq on the same date.

Over the next two days, thirty-one B-52G sorties launched from the United States struck Republican Guard elements as well as the Tawakalna Mechanized Infantry Division, beginning a pattern of the B-52Gs being tasked with attacking Iraqi ground forces. The targets, like those being attacked by other Coalition aircraft, were designated within specific "kill boxes" that were overlaid on known Iraqi troop concentrations inside Kuwait.

The Coalition Combined OPLAN (Operational Plan), and the USCINCCENT (Commander in Chief, CENTCOM) OPLAN called for "continuous B-52 strikes, TACAIR (tactical air) attacks, and attack helicopter operations." In anticipation

■ A close-up view of M117 750-pound bombs loaded into the bomb bay of a B-52G prior to a bombing mission during Operation Desert Storm. *DoD photo, PH3 Chester Falkenhainer*

■ A B-52G of the 1708th Provisional Bombardment Wing, armed with Mk 82 500-pound bombs, takes off from Prince Abdulla AB in Saudi Arabia. *USAF photo, Sgt. Donald McMichael*

■ A B-52G takes off from RAF Fairford on a mission during Operation Desert Storm. *USAF photo, Senior Airman Chris Putman*

■ A B-52G of the 410th Bombardment Wing from K. I. Sawyer AFB, Michigan, armed with Mk 82 500-pound bombs on the wing pylons. *USAF photo, Sgt. Donald McMichael*

of the eventual ground offensive, "The bridges, roads and rail line. . . will be cut to block withdrawal of [Iraqi Republican Guard troops] and to form a kill zone north of Kuwait."

While the first missions originated from Barksdale AFB and Diego Garcia, other early missions were also flown from Wurtsmith AFB in Michigan. On the first day of the air campaign, the Spanish government approved offensive operations from its Morón AB, which is roughly the same distance from Kuwait as Diego Garcia. On January 18, ten B-52Gs flying from Wurtsmith AFB, deployed to Morón after striking their targets in Kuwait.

While the Coalition and the United Nations mandate for Operation Desert Storm brought an almost limitless level of support for the Gulf War from most countries in Europe and the Middle East, when it came to the mighty Stratofortress, there was a great deal of reticence. As Thomas Keaney and Eliot Cohen write in the *Gulf War Air Power Survey Summary Report*, "There were some exceptions to this unprecedented extension of staging and overflight rights, most notably the basing of B-52s requiring bases with

Left: A view of the roll control spoiler panel with one of the flaps torn off on the wing of a B-52G from the 1708th Bombardment Wing and other battle damage sustained during Operation Desert Storm. *USAF photo, Sergeant Rose Reynolds* ▪ Right: On a mission during Operation Desert Storm, two SAC B-52G Stratofortresses prepare to take off from Prince Abdulla AB at Jeddah in Saudi Arabia. *USAF photo, Sgt. Rose Reynolds*

extensive runway and ramp operating areas and access to specialized logistical support. The stationing of B-52s overseas raised political concerns for several potential host nations. Throughout the aircraft's history, host foreign governments had allowed B-52 basing only under limited conditions because of the B-52s' link with nuclear weapons and their widely publicized role in the Vietnam War. These restrictions and the concerns that drove them proved resistant to change.

"During Desert Shield, the U.S. Air Force proposed B-52 basing in several countries, including Egypt, Saudi Arabia, and Spain, but no moves took place until the air campaign began. It is unclear who was more reluctant: the potential host governments or American officials who did not wish to press them on a potentially delicate issue at a time when weightier matters appeared to be at stake. Certainly the base in Saudi Arabia proposed for B-52 basing raised such concerns, given that Iraq had already accused Saudi Arabia of allowing Westerners to desecrate the Muslim holy places. To minimize the problem, B-52s deployed to their wartime operating bases, but with no publicity and only after the air campaign began. Some B-52s flying from Diego Garcia or Wurtsmith AFB in the United States landed in the theater after the initial attacks of the air campaign."

Of course, the Iraqis had proven in Kuwait that "desecration" was the least of the hardships imposed upon the people in a country that *they* occupied.

In fact, B-52s did operate out of Saudi Arabia during the Gulf War. The 1708th Provisional Bombardment Wing was formed at Prince Abdulla AB in Jeddah in August 1990 and was composed of B-52Gs and crews from several Stateside squadrons. One of these aircraft flew twenty-nine missions, the most of any Stratofortress in the war.

In addition, small numbers of BUFFs were also attached to SAC's 1701st and 1703rd Provisional Air Refueling Wings at Jeddah and King Khalid Military City, respectively.

In the meantime, Turkey also authorized United States air operations from its territory, and these began on the second day of the air war. These were effectively a forward deployment by the United States Air Forces in Europe, which operated under the umbrella of the 7440th Composite Wing, also called Joint Task Force (JTF) Proven Force, and which did not include any Stratofortresses among its assets. These aircraft operated against targets within Iraq from to Incirlik AB.

On February 2, the *New York Times* announced "France agrees to allow American B-52s based in Britain to enter its airspace for raids against Iraq, and to refuel at a French military base enroute."

The base in Britain was RAF Fairford, a Royal Air Force base in Gloucestershire, which had hosted American units since World War II and SAC bombers since 1950. It had not been used prior to February because routing the strike missions around French airspace would have been a distance greater than that from Moròn or Diego Garcia. The 806th Provisional Bombardment Wing was formed at Fairford to operate these BUFFs. Secretary of Defense Dick Cheney ordered them to fly against targets inside Iraq in support of JTF Proven Force, while the Diego Garcia– and Moròn-based BUFFs targeted Kuwait and southern Iraq.

On February 3, with eight BUFFs operating out of Fairford, Cheney ordered an additional dozen B-52Gs to Moròn. By February 6, the U.S. Air Force noted a total of seventy-one Stratofortresses supporting Desert Storm. A total of 457 strike sorties had been flown in January, and the Air Force reported that "the current daily sortie rate for the B-52s exceeds the highest previously planned wartime rates."

The B-52Gs were also used to drop armor-sensing mines, and three BUFFs were diverted to attack an armored column during the Iraqi assault on the Saudi town of Al-Khafji on January 31. Other BUFF missions were tasked against strategic targets within Iraq itself, such as the military production plant at Habbaniyah in Al-Anbar Province, near Baghdad. On January 29, B-52Gs struck the ammunition storage facility at Ar-Rumaylah near Basra in southern Iraq, setting off an immense explosion that the Department of Defense *Final Report* colorfully describes as "the equivalent of an erupting volcano."

As a counterpoint to the effectiveness of the American strategic bomber, Saddam Hussein turned to his arsenal of tactical ballistic missiles, including Soviet-made R-300/SS-1c Scud-B weapons and home-built knock offs. Striking their targets without warning at supersonic speeds, the Scuds delivered a fear factor that went beyond their questionable tactical usefulness. On January 22, when a Scud hit a residential area in Tel Aviv, killing three Israelis, CENTAF diverted considerable resources to prevent the Scud menace from widening the war to include Israel. Because they are launched from mobile launchers, the Scuds were hard to find and presented a perplexing problem for Coalition air power. B-52Gs were among the assets diverted to attacking suspected Scud "hide sites" and support facilities at airfields in western Iraq.

A crew from the 1708th Bombardment Wing's aircraft battle damage repair section works on a battle damaged B-52G. *USAF photo, Sgt. Rose Reynolds*

Coalition air power struck at night as well as by day. In the Department of Defense *Final Report*, it is noted that "the Coalition's ability to fight at night made it difficult for the Iraqis to use the cover of darkness to maintain and repair equipment, and replenish supplies. This was a key advantage helping to keep pressure on the Iraqis 24 hours a day."

The Gulf War was fought by generals who had been front-line captains in Vietnam, and an important historical subtext to their strategic thinking was not to make many of the mistakes that had been made in the 1960s. To begin with, the Gulf War was not fought as a "sublimited war," nor were minute tactical details micromanaged from Washington, as they had been by the Johnson administration.

However, in one sense, the Gulf War was like the Vietnam War, and this was with respect to the deployment of the B-52 force. In Vietnam, the strategic Stratofortresses were tasked with tactical Arc Light missions in the south, while tactical fighter-bombers flew ostensibly strategic Rolling Thunder missions against North Vietnam. In the Gulf War, the principal use of the BUFF was against troop concentrations.

The back story to this decision was articulated by Lt. Col. David Deptula. An original member of the famed "Black Hole" strategic planning group, he was the principal deputy for strategic targeting to CENTCOM war plans chief Maj. Gen. Buster Glosson. In a December 1991 interview for the *Gulf War Air Power Survey* Project, he recalled that "attempts by air planners to employ B-52Gs outside the Kuwait theater (on munitions storage sites in Iraq, for example) ran into much opposition from the CENTCOM leadership, particularly General Schwarzkopf. Army and Marine commanders, meanwhile, had restricted the employment of attack helicopters until the approach of the ground war."

In their *Gulf War Air Power Survey Summary Report*, Keaney and Cohen write that "Tensions between the Air Force and American ground commanders persisted because the commanders did not understand that many decisions causing them problems were Schwarzkopf's and not Horner's. Sometimes Schwarzkopf's decisions did please the ground commanders. For example, they liked to see B-52s dropping bombs in front of their positions, and Schwarzkopf often obliged. As [Marine Corps] General [Walter] Boomer noted later, ground commanders like himself had been closer to B-52 strikes in Vietnam than any Air Force officer and knew their psychological impact first hand. Schwarzkopf ordered extensive B-52 bombing of Iraqi troops (who were dispersed and dug in) despite reservations on the part of Air Force officers who preferred to use the big bombers against more vulnerable area targets like supply depots."

Keaney and Cohen go on to add that the BUFF did become "one of the most sought-after aircraft by the ground commanders for strikes against Iraqi ground forces."

■ Sergeant Brian Land checks a .50-caliber tail turret gun on a B-52G. While two BUFF tail gunners scored kills during Operation Linebacker II in 1972, no kills were scored with tail guns in Operation Desert Storm nineteen years later. *USAF photo, Chief Master Sgt. Don Sutherland*

■ A view of the battle damaged tail section of a B-52G from the 1708th Bombardment Wing. *USAF photo, Sgt. Rose Reynolds*

■ A B-52G from the 1708th Bombardment Wing at Prince Abdulla AB in Saudi Arabia is prepared for a mission. *USAF photo, Sgt. Donald McMichael*

A B-52G takes off on March 10, 1991, for its return flight to the United States after being deployed for Operation Desert Storm. The first Gulf War saw the longest strike mission in the history of aerial warfare when BUFFs took off from Barksdale AFB in Louisiana, fired AGM-86C Conventional Air-Launched Cruise Missiles on Iraqi forces, and returned to Barksdale, thirty-five hours later. *USAF photo, Sgt. Donald McMichael*

As had been the case during Arc Light operations in Vietnam, the ability of the BUFF to release an immense bomb load on a relatively compact target area had a devastating effect on enemy morale. This was taken into account by air and ground commanders alike.

Volant Solo psychological warfare operations took advantage of this fact. For example, on January 29, Volant Solo EC-130s flew over the positions of the Iraqi 20th Infantry Division ahead of the BUFF strikes dropping "personalized" leaflets that warned them of the incoming attacks. As noted in the U.S. Air Force *Gulf War Air Power Survey*, the leaflets read "If you want to live, leave now. Do not allow anyone to stop you. Save yourself by fleeing south. If you choose to stay, you choose death."

The next day, after the B-52G strikes, the EC-130s dropped more leaflets. These read "We told you that you were to be bombed and you were. We are telling you again that you will be bombed tomorrow. Leave now. Flee south or die."

As noted in the Department of Defense *Final Report*, senior Iraqi officers who were captured and debriefed after the war "frequently commented their troops also were terrified of B-52Gs, and could clearly see and hear their strikes, even when miles away."

One such officer told American intelligence personnel that he surrendered only because of B-52G strikes.

"But your position was never attacked by B-52Gs," his interrogator replied.

"That is true," the Iraqi officer stated, "but I saw one that had been attacked."

By the latter half of February, the Coalition air power was thoroughly involved in paving the way for the ground offensive, which was scheduled for the end of the month.

As the *Gulf War Air Power Survey* notes, General Schwarzkopf's CENTCOM headquarters confirmed on February 16 that "battlefield preparations, to include mine breaching by B-52s, will remain the primary focus of the air war."

To this end, B-52Gs bombed the minefields with M117 bombs, as well as 500-pound Mk 82 bombs, while MC-130s dropped 15,000-pound BLU-82 "daisy-cutter" bombs to create over-pressure and detonate mines.

On "G-Day," February 24, the thirty-ninth day of the air war, the Coalition launched the long-awaited offensive ground campaign to liberate Kuwait. As the Defense Department *Final Report* states, around three thousand air sorties were flown, including "more than 1,200 against armor, artillery and infantry, and others against 'selected' airfields, bridges, arms plants, nuclear-biological-chemical and command, control, and communications sites. . . Forty-three B-52G struck Iraqi defenses and infantry positions in the Kuwait Theater of Operations."

According to Keaney and Cohen in *Gulf War Air Power Survey*, *Summary Report*, the "B-52s flew around the clock: on the first day, they hit breaching sites and front line forces; on subsequent days they struck headquarters and staging areas just south of the Euphrates River in Iraq. The plan intended to put maximum pressure on the Iraqi forces with every type of strike aircraft at the Coalition's disposal."

Thanks to the air campaign and its thorough preparation of the battlefield, the ground aspect of Operation Desert Storm lasted but four days. Iraqi forces in Kuwait resisted, but the resistance was quickly overcome. The Iraqis surrendered, and a ceasefire went into effect at 0500 on February 28, 1991.

Keaney and Cohen note that the B-52Gs flew 457 strike sorties in January and 1,188 in February, for a total of 1,645. In their "Listing of Selected Munitions Employed in Desert Storm" they mention that the Stratofortresses dropped 43,435 tons of M117s alone.

Several BUFFs suffered damage from antiaircraft fire, including one that lost much of its tail to an SA-3 SAM. One B-52G was hit by an AGM-88A HARM missile in a friendly fire incident. Only a single BUFF was lost in the Gulf War, but it was officially not due to enemy fire. While returning from a mission, this aircraft suffered a catastrophic electrical failure and crashed into the Indian Ocean about 17 miles northwest of Diego Garcia, killing three of the six crew members on board. Some sources say that battle damage was at least a contributing factor in the loss.

Desert Storm had seen the BUFF's first sustained combat operations since 1972, and one might extrapolate from the statistical data that the B-52 might be considered to have been the single most important strike aircraft type in the Coalition arsenal.

As Keaney and Cohen summarize, the Stratofortresses dropped "approximately thirty-two percent of the bomb tonnage in the war (most of it in the Kuwait theater), attacked area targets (breaching sites, ammunition stockpiles, troop concentrations, and military field headquarters) and became one of the most sought-after aircraft by the ground commanders for strikes against Iraqi ground forces."

=10= A Decade of Changes

THE B-52GS RETURNED from Desert Storm to accept their scheduled retirement from service. Though this had been delayed by the Gulf War, it was accelerated when the Strategic Arms Reduction Treaty (START) was signed by President George H. W. Bush and Soviet President Mikhail Gorbachev on July 31, 1991. START called for the entire B-52G fleet to be scrapped, and this was done in dramatic fashion.

All of the venerable aircraft were flown to the Aerospace Maintenance and Regeneration Center (AMARC), the site at Arizona's Davis-Monthan AFB previously known as the Military Aircraft Storage and Disposition Center (MASDC). Here, they were stripped of usable parts and chopped into five pieces by a "guillotine," a 13,000-pound steel blade dropped from a crane that cut off the wings and chopped each fuselage into three pieces. From a total of 230 B-52Gs and B-52Hs at the end of 1990, the fleet was reduced to just 85 B-52Hs by the end of 1994, a force level that would remain constant for more than a decade.

In September 1991, two months after signing START and seven months after the Gulf War, Bush ordered the Strategic Air Command to stand down the continuous strategic alert that its bomber and ICBM crews had been on for nearly four decades. No longer would B-52 crews be primed to fly a nuclear strike mission with fifteen-minute notice.

At the same time, Bush ordered a reorganization of the post–Cold War U.S. Air Force, which included the consolidation of the warfighting commands and the elimination of SAC itself—something that would have been unthinkable just a few years earlier.

Effective on May 31, 1992, the functions, units, personnel, and combat aircraft of both SAC and TAC were consolidated into a single Air Combat Command (ACC), with SAC's ICBM force going to the Air Force Space Command (AFSPC). Most of SAC's tanker fleet was merged with the transport aircraft fleet of the Military Airlift Command (MAC) into the new Air Mobility Command (AMC). Nine B-52Hs were transferred to the Air Force Reserve (AFRES)—Air Force Reserve Command (AFRC) after 1997—the first time that Stratofortresses served with the reserve force.

Meanwhile, the Defense Department formed a new joint command to manage the nuclear strike assets of both the U.S. Navy and Air Force. This organization, the United States Strategic Command (USSTRATCOM), would take over the former SAC headquarters at Offutt AFB, Nebraska. Ironically, Curtis LeMay had proposed such a merger in 1959, but met resistance from the U.S. Navy. The first commander of STRATCOM, was Gen. George Butler, SAC's last commander.

A December 1993 view of B-52G and B-52D aircraft parked in storage at the 309th Aerospace Maintenance and Regeneration Group boneyard at Davis-Monthan AFB in Arizona. *USAF photo, Sgt. John McDowell*

As the Damocles Sword of nuclear war was perceived as finally removed, and veteran B-52Gs beaten into plowshares, an era came to an end.

In the United States, defense spending declined, and there were those in government who spoke naively of a "Peace Dividend," as though the end of the Cold War meant an end to all threats to "peace." Of course, despite the lifting of the Damocles Sword, the 1990s were, if anything, less peaceful for American armed forces than the 1970s or 1980s had been.

The remaining B-52Hs, which had yet to be in combat as the decade began, finally had a brief baptism of fire in 1996 during Operation Desert Strike. In response to Saddam Hussein's brutal repression of an uprising by the Kurdish minority around

■ The USAF's Air Combat Command (ACC) was created on June 1, 1992, by combining the aircraft and personnel of the Strategic Air Command and the Tactical Air Command. In 2010, control of nuclear-capable strategic bombers, including the BUFF, was moved from ACC to the newly constituted Air Force Global Strike Command (AFGSC). *USAF*

■ United States Strategic Command was created on June 1, 1992 as one of nine Unified Combatant Commands of the United States Department of Defense. It was seen as a successor to SAC, in that it took over control of SAC's strategic nuclear strike and strategic reconnaissance assets, as well as SAC's former headquarters at Offutt AFB. *DoD*

■ A pair of B-52Hs on a training mission over a western bombing range. *USAF*

Two visiting Tupolev Tu-95 Bear bomber aircraft, center, and an Antonov An-124 Condor transport aircraft of the Russian military, background, are parked on the Barksdale AFB flight line beside a B-52H of the 62nd Bombardment Squadron in May 1992. The Bear originated in the early 1950s concurrently with the B-52, and with its 35-degree wing sweep and turboprop engines driving contra-rotating propellers, it was seen by some as a knockoff of Boeing's early Model 464 proposals. *USAF photo, Sgt. Fernando Serna*

Urbil in northern Iraq, the United States launched a series of air attacks on September 3. As part of the strike package, two B-52Hs from the 2nd Bombardment Wing launched from Andersen AFB on Guam and attacked air defense sites in southern Iraq with thirteen AGM-86C CALCMs. Parenthetically, one year earlier, on August 25, 1995, a B-52H from the same wing had set a new speed record for aircraft of its weight class, flying eleven hours twenty-three minutes unrefueled, with an average speed of 556 miles per hour.

Stand-Off Missiles, the Third Generation

Among the new weapons systems being developed as the Cold War came to a close was General Dynamics (later Raytheon) AGM-129 Advanced Cruise Missile (ACM). Nearly identical in size and weight to the AGM-86 ALCM, it incorporated stealth characteristics and had a longer range of 2,300 miles. The initial acquisition plan for 2,500 ACMs was scaled back several times and terminated in 1993 after about 460 AGM-129As were delivered. Long assumed to be the successor to the AGM-86 family, the ACM would be phased out in 2007, leaving the ALCM still in the U.S. Air Force inventory.

Another weapon acquired to extend the conventional stand-off reach of the Stratofortress was the AGM-142, which was derived from the Popeye missile developed in Israel by Rafael Advanced Defense Systems. It was adapted for the U.S. Air Force by Precision Guided Systems, a joint venture of Rafael and Lockheed Martin, under the Have Nap program. Weighing 3,000 pounds, the AGM-142 is 15 feet 10 inches long. The generally similar variants include the AGM-142A with an electro-optical seeker, the AGM-142B with an infrared seeker, the AGM-142C with an electro-optical seeker and a

A dramatic studio image of the AGM-158 joint air-to-surface stand-off missile (JASSM). *Lockheed Martin*

An AGM-129 advanced cruise missile during an early test flight.

hardened target penetrating warhead, and the AGM-142D with an infrared seeker and the penetrating warhead. The U.S. Air Force acquired its first 154 AGM-142s in 1989, but would not use them in combat until 2001.

The AGM-142 was originally acquired only for the B-52G, because its Heavy Stores Adapter Beams (HSAB) gave it the carrying capacity that was lacking in the B-52H. In 1994, after the scrapping of the B-52Gs, the B-52Hs underwent a Conventional Enhancement Modification (CEM), which fitted them with HSABs to permit them to carry and fire a broad range of conventional weapons. In addition to the AGM-142, the B-52H could now carry the AGM-84 Harpoon, as well as the AGM-84E Stand-off Land Attack Missile (SLAM), and the AGM-154 Joint Stand-Off Weapon (JSOW). Recently included in the BUFF's arsenal is the Lockheed Martin AGM-158 Joint Air-to-Surface Stand-off Missile (JASSM), which entered service in 2009.

Enter JDAM

At a time when complex air-launched weapons systems such as the AGM-86 ALCM and CALCM, as well as the AGM-129 and AGM-142, were garnering a great deal of attention, a less-heralded air-launched weapon was making its way through the development process. The Joint Direct Attack Munition (JDAM) program was initiated in 1992 in response to the experiences of pilots flying ground attack missions in poor weather during Operation Desert Storm in 1991. The idea was to develop a relatively inexpensive and uncomplicated way to convert existing unguided free-fall "dumb" bombs into accurate, "smart" munitions usable in adverse weather. The result was a kit that includes a new tail section containing a Global Positioning System (GPS) and Inertial Navigation System (INS) for a guidance control unit.

The first JDAM kits were the GBU-31, designed for use with 2,000-pound BLU-109 and Mk 84 bombs, and the GBU-32, for 1,000-pound BLU-110 and Mk 83 weapons. In 1999, Boeing introduced the GBU-38 JDAM kit for the Mk 82 500-pound bomb.

The first deliveries came in 1998, and the total numbers delivered reached 200,000 within a decade. The large quantity is attributable to the success of the JDAM concept as seen during Operation Allied Force in 1999.

Allied Force

At the end of the 1990s, the United States became involved in a North Atlantic Treaty Organization (NATO) intervention in the Balkans during the collapse of the Federal Republic of Yugoslavia. Through the decade, most of the major components of the "former Yugoslavia," such as Croatia and Slovenia, had peeled off to form independent countries. Serbia, still calling itself Yugoslavia, had earned the ire of the international community

Three B-52 Stratofortresses from Barksdale AFB taxi to the runway at RAF Fairford for an Allied Force mission. *USAF*

A B-52H from the 2nd Bombardment Wing trails a drag chute upon landing at RAF Fairford in the United Kingdom. In October 1998, the wing forward-deployed five aircraft in support of possible strikes against Serbian targets. *Sgt. James Howard*

through the tactics it used—ranging from ethnic cleansing to mere bloodshed—to forestall the toppling of dominos that marked Yugoslav disintegration. By 1998, Serbian/Yugoslav president Slobodan Milosevic was fighting a deadly war to keep Kosovo in the fold, using especially fierce brutality against the Kosovo Liberation Army (KLA) insurgents and the people of Kosovo.

During the summer of 1998, there were calls for NATO to intervene with military air power, as they had for a month in 1995 during the Serbian ethnic cleansing of Bosnia and Herzegovina. NATO defense ministers initiated contingency planning for such a move, and U.S. Secretary of Defense William Cohen ordered a buildup of American air power in the region similar to that which took place in 1995 in preparation for Operation Deliberate Force.

On October 8, 1998, Deputy Secretary of Defense Dr. John Hamre promised that the U.S. Air Force would deploy its ultimate bomber, the "very expensive" B-2A Spirit stealth bomber as part of the strike package. Two days later, Cohen also ordered the

■ An airman secures an AGM-84C CALCM aboard a B-52H at RAF Fairford on March 25, 1999. Note that the tail gun has been removed from this BUFF. *USAF photo, Sgt. James Howard*

■ A B-52 Stratofortress, from the 5th Bombardment Wing, Minot AFB, takes off, homeward bound, on June 23, 1999, after supporting Operation Allied Force. *USAF photo, Sgt. James Howard*

■ A B-52H of the 2nd Air Expeditionary Group heads toward a target in Kosovo on May 26, 1999, during an Operation Allied Force mission. *USAF photo, Senior Airman Greg Davis*

■ This spectacular photograph shows a B-52H moments before it crashed at Fairchild AFB during low-level aerobatics on June 24, 1994. The copilot's escape hatch has been jettisoned, but none of the crew escaped. *USAF*

deployment of six B-52Hs from the 2nd Bombardment Wing at Barksdale AFB to RAF Fairford in the United Kingdom, from which B-52Gs had flown against targets in Iraq seven years earlier. Two more arrived on February 22, 1999, as NATO slowly prepared for "possible contingency operations" in Kosovo.

On March 24, NATO finally launched the air operation against Serbia, designated as Operation Allied Force. Among the roughly 210 American aircraft involved were four of the B-52Hs. The USAFE News Service reported that "the bombers launched and headed home to Louisiana after participating in the first wave of air strikes over the former Republic of Yugoslavia."

The BUFFs were not alone among the aircraft of the former SAC. According to the Air Force Print News agency, "When five B-1B bombers were ordered to deploy to

Europe March 29 in support of NATO operations in Yugoslavia, it marked a milestone in modern bomber history. Operation Allied Force is the first time the Air Force's heavy bomber fleet—the B-2 Spirit, B-52H Stratofortress and B-1B Lancer—are being used together operationally."

At the end of April, the BUFF fleet was augmented by an additional eight from Barksdale and two from the 5th Bombardment Wing at Minot AFB in North Dakota, which deployed to Fairford on April 29. According to a Defense Department briefing the same day, the B-52Hs were armed with CALCMs, as well as "a variety of other weapons." These included AGM-129 ACMs and AGM-142 Have Nap precision-guided munitions. The Defense Department briefer specifically noted that "five of the B-52Hs that we are sending over, of this new batch of B-52Hs, are outfitted to fire the Have Nap."

Slobodan Milosevic discovered in 1999, as Saddam Hussein discovered in 1991 and as Adolf Hitler discovered in 1944, that a sustained aerial bombardment campaign can take a serious toll on a nation's ability to wage war. As the Viet Cong and the Iraqi Republican Guard on the front lines had discovered, the awesome power of a B-52's bomb load is a horrible thing to endure, and experiencing it firsthand is a horrible way to make that discovery.

By the end of May 1999, the BUFF had established its reputation among the ethnic cleansers of the Serbian army. On May 30, the BBC repeated a report from the Serbian news agency Beta that NATO aircraft "had dropped leaflets over the Kosovo capital Pristina urging Serbian troops to desert their units and leave or face bombardment by B-52 bombers."

A B-52H from the 96th Bombardment Squadron, deployed to the 2nd Air Expeditionary Group on Diego Garcia in November 1998 as part of Operation Desert Thunder, a force buildup for possible action against Iraq in response to attempted Iraqi interceptions of American reconnaissance aircraft.
USAF photo, Senior Airman Sarah Shaw, USAF Photo

A close-up view of a B-52H as it makes a bomb drop in August 1995. The BUFF from the 96th Bombardment Squadron set a record for flying, unrefueled, and with a payload of 5,000 kilograms, from Edwards AFB to Greenland and back.
USAF photo, Richard Kemp

According to the BBC, the Serbian-language leaflets read "The Yugoslav Army forces are warned to leave Kosovo, because NATO is now using B-52 bombers to cast Mk 82 bombs, weighing 225 kilograms each. . . . Every B-52 bomber can carry more than 50 such bombs. These aircraft will be after you until they drive you out of Kosovo. . . and prevent you from committing atrocities. . . . If you want to survive and see your families again, you should abandon your units and firearms."

Also by this time, the beleaguered Milosevic had been entertaining thoughts of a negotiated end to his occupation of Kosovo, though he found it hard to let go of one more dominion that had been part of the Serb-dominated Yugoslavia for more than eight decades. Like the North Vietnamese on the eve of Linebacker II, Milosevic was a reluctant negotiator, hoping that his adversary would run out of steam and leave him alone.

Slobodan Milosevic's Linebacker II moment came on the first weekend of June 1999 at a place on the Kosovo-Albania border called Mount Pastrik. Here, the KLA was fighting a sizable Serbian army force. As NATO commander Gen. Wesley Clark told his subordinate commanders via video conferencing, "That mountain is not going to get lost. I'm not going to have Serbs on that mountain. We'll pay for that hill with American blood if we don't help [the KLA] hold it."

On Sunday, June 6, CNN reported that "NATO used B-52 bombers Saturday night into Sunday to strike areas in Kosovo near its border with Albania. There was also military activity along the border between Albania and Kosovo. NATO used B-52 bombers to strike an area near Gorshub in Yugoslavia, just inside the border. The mountain plateau was also the scene of a day-long artillery and mortar battle between Yugoslav forces and the KLA."

On Wednesday, June 9, Reuters reported that "a NATO B-52 bomber caught two Yugoslav Army battalions in the open after Serbia stalled on pulling its troops out of Kosovo and many hundreds of troops may have been killed, alliance sources said Tuesday. The B-52 dropped sticks of gravity bombs on the troop concentrations near the Kosovo-Albania border Monday, carpeting a hillside area where some 400 to 800 soldiers were estimated to have been in the field."

Reuters added that NATO military spokesman Gen. Walter Jertz confirmed that "heavy bombers had been diverted at short notice to attack troops in Kosovo."

When asked if the alliance had been pulling its punches while top-level diplomatic moves were under way, NATO spokesman Jamie Shea replied that "I'm sure that if you were in the field in Kosovo in the Yugoslav Army yesterday you wouldn't have perceived this as holding back at all. The pressure was very intense, particularly in the sorties that were carried out by the B-52s against the Serb fielded forces in the Mount Pastrik area."

Also on June 9, Dana Priest of the *Washington Post* wrote that "at least a month ago, NATO commanders began using B-52s to herd troops on the ground into more open and vulnerable areas (because there are no NATO troops on the ground to do this). In the last two weeks, B-52s and B-1Bs have been deployed against the massing of Serb forces that has occurred in response to a KLA rebel offensive along the Albanian border. NATO has used this opportunity to take out large numbers of troops that were, in essence, hiding from them before. On Monday, a pair of B-52s and B-1Bs dropped 86 Mk 82s. . . on a concentration of several hundred Serb troops near the Mt. Pastrik region."

On June 10, NATO ratified the terms of an international peace plan and suspended the seventy-eight-day air campaign. Two days later, in Dana Priest's words, "Slobodan Milosevic unexpectedly capitulated. . . . Milosevic signed an agreement allowing the invasion of 50,000 NATO soldiers—but as peacekeepers, not warriors."

The NATO-led peacekeeping Kosovo Force (KFOR) began entering Kosovo, which was now under UN administration. KFOR had planned for combat operations, but was now going in only in a peacekeeping role.

Slobodan Milosevic resigned as president after a disputed presidential election in September 2000 and was arrested by Yugoslav federal authorities in March 2001 on charges ranging from corruption to embezzlement. Sent to The Hague to stand trial for war crimes, he died in March 2006 before his interminable trial reached a verdict.

For the BUFF, the Kosovo War ended in a moment of triumph with the venerable warhorse having played a small, but pivotal, role in the climactic moment.

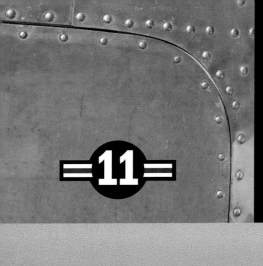

11 Twenty-First-Century Warrior

N THE 1980s, it was often said that few people could have realistically predicted in the 1960s that the Stratofortress would still be in front line service in the 1980s. To this, it is obvious to add that few of those in the 1980s would have realistically predicted that the BUFF would be in front-line combat in the twenty-first century. Nor would most people have predicted that from March 2000 through March 2001, the mission capable rate for the Stratofortress was 80.5 percent, compared with 53.7 percent for the B-1B and 30.3 percent for the B-2A.

Of course, few people in the twentieth century could have predicted many things about what happened during and after September 2001.

Enduring Freedom

September 11, 2001—like December 7, 1941—was a day of infamy that changed the course of American history. The coordinated hijackings of four jetliners by Osama bin Laden's al-Qaeda terrorist network destroyed the twin towers of New York's World Trade Center, damaged the Pentagon, and killed 2,977 people in three states. These previously unimaginable attacks both shocked the nation and invited retaliatory action.

The focus was on Afghanistan, where the Islamist Taliban regime had been providing safe haven for bin Laden and his gang. The United States issued an ultimatum demanding the Taliban turn in the al-Qaeda leadership, close down terrorist training camps, and allow U.S. access to the camps for confirmation. When the Taliban rejected the ultimatum on September 21, the United States prepared for action, which was to be initiated under the umbrella of the Global War on Terror (GWOT).

On October 7, the United States began the GWOT with Operation Enduring Freedom, a military offensive aimed at crushing al-Qaeda and removing the Taliban from power in Afghanistan.

As in Desert Storm a decade earlier, and the subsequent limited air operations over Iraq in the 1990s, overall command of the operation was with the United States Central Command (CENTCOM), now under U.S. Army Gen. Tommy Franks. The air component (CENTAF) was under the command of Lt. Gen. Charles Wald and was managed from CENTCOM's forward-based Combined Air Operations Center (CAOC) at Prince Sultan Air Base in Saudi Arabia.

The strategy for Enduring Freedom, as summarized in the RAND Corporation after-action assessment was "to rely on air power and precision weapons, aided on the ground by U.S. Special Operations Forces (SOF), who would work alongside indigenous Afghan groups [specifically the Northern Alliance] opposed to the Taliban and identify and validate targets for allied aircrews."

Operating from Diego Garcia in the Indian Ocean, the B-52H was part of the opening phase of the Enduring Freedom air campaign, which involved sorties by carrier-based U.S. Navy aircraft, as well as U.S. Air Force B-1B Lancers, and B-2A Spirits. Initial targets included radar and command and control facilities, but the target list expanded over the subsequent days to include airfields and aircraft.

Bomber and aerial refueling operations out of Diego Garcia were under the umbrella of the 40th Air Expeditionary Wing (later 40th Air Expeditionary Group), which was reactivated on Diego Garcia in October 2001. Created as a bombardment group during

■ Ground crew members wave at a B-52H as it prepares for takeoff from Diego Garcia for a strike mission against al-Qaeda in Afghanistan on October 7, 2001.

USAF photo, Senior Airman Rebeca Luquin

■ A B-52H of the 2nd Bombardment Wing, Barksdale AFB, Louisiana, wears "Let's Roll" commemorative nose art. "Let's Roll," was the famous phrase used by United Airlines Flight 93 passenger Todd Beamer as he and fellow passengers attacked terrorist hijackers on September 11, 2001.

USAF photo, Sgt. Denise Rayder

World War II, it had evolved into the 40th Tactical Wing and had been deactivated in 1992. The B-52Hs assigned to the wing were drawn from the 2nd Bombardment Wing at Barksdale AFB, and the 5th Bombardment Wing at Minot AFB. Meanwhile, B-1Bs deployed overseas under the 28th Air Expeditionary Wing.

Sgt. Kathleen Rhem of the American Forces Press Service was on hand to interview the Air Force bomber pilots returning after the first night of operations. A B-52H radar operator called "Doc" told her that "the president counted on us to do a job, and the [American] people counted on us to do a job tonight. Whether you're from Manhattan or the Washington, D.C. area, it doesn't really matter. We're all Americans, and we're all in this together."

Nearby, Rhem noticed the slogan "NYPD—We Remember," a reference to New York police officers killed on September 11.

"It all came together because we train for this," a B-52 pilot nicknamed "Woodstock" told the journalist. "This is what the American citizens expect us to be able to do, and in peacetime we prepare for these eventualities. [From the intelligence information to the ground crews, it came together like a] finely oiled machine."

The first bomber attacks were by night, but as Air Force Capt. Gregory Ball notes in an official overview of the campaign, "On the second day of the air offensive, coalition aircraft began operating during the day; and by the tenth day of operations, planners established 'target zones' throughout Afghanistan to. . . engage targets of opportunity around the clock, because the Taliban's air defenses were negligible."

By the end of October, the B-52Hs were concentrating their immense bomb loads on Taliban and al-Qaeda ground forces and infrastructure, especially troop concentrations in the area of Bagram AB near Kabul and Mazar-e-Sharif, north of Kabul, the fourth-largest city of Afghanistan. Ball notes that in the capture of Mazar-e-Sharif on November 9, the use of air power "was considered a major breakthrough in the struggle to oust the Taliban and al-Qaeda."

The bomb capacity of the former SAC bombers, especially the Stratofortress, made them, pound for pound, the most important aircraft of the air campaign. Through October 23, the three U.S. Air Force bomber types had dropped in excess of 80 percent of the bomb tonnage targeting Afghanistan, though they were flying just a tenth of the total sorties. Through the end of November, just eight B-1Bs and ten B-52Hs operating from Diego Garcia had dropped 72 percent of total tonnage. In the first seventy-six days of operations, from October 7 to December 23, when the pace slowed, B-1A and B-52H bombers had dropped 11,500 of the 17,500 total munitions delivered. The U.S. Air Force reported that the B-52Hs were averaging five missions a day, compared with four daily for the B-1Bs.

The bombers were directed to targets in real time by ground-based Special Forces Joint Terminal Attack Controllers (JTACs), Forward Air Controllers (FACs), or by airborne "Fast FACs" in jet fighters, all using precision GPS targeting.

The BUFF proved to be a vital weapon in Enduring Freedom, not only for its ordnance capacity, but for its endurance. As attested to by the circling contrails seen from the ground, the BUFFs spent a great deal of time over the theater, waiting to be called in to a specific target. Indeed, some missions lasted for up to fifteen hours as the BUFFs loitered over Afghanistan. The fact that B-52Hs had the staying power to be able to do this gave them an advantage over smaller tactical aircraft, which required more frequent refuelings.

Precision-guided weapons also allowed the BUFFs be used more effectively than ever for ground support. As Dr. Carlo Kopp writes in his *Operation Enduring Freedom Analysis*, "the heavy bombers could orbit for hours picking off targets on demand. Different targets could be optimally attacked with varying numbers of guided or unguided weapons. Unlike fighters, limited in weapons loads and mixes by payload limitations, a B-52H/B-1B bomber could either pick off point targets with single JDAMs, obliterate a trenchline with Mk 82/Mk 84 or demolish a group of buildings or bunkers with multiple Mk 84 or BLU-109/B 2,000 pounders."

Citing advances in precision munitions, notably the JDAM, Tommy Franks reported that an average of two hundred daily sorties "hit roughly the same number of targets hit with 3,000 sorties" in Operation Desert Storm.

As Dr. Rebecca Grant pointed out in *Air Force Magazine* in September 2002, "both the B-1 and B-52 now carried GPS-guided Joint Direct Attack Munitions. For the first time in combat, these bombers followed the lead of the B-2s in Allied Force in 1999 and linked into the net of updated information to take new target coordinates in real time. Bombers generally did not have their entire load of weapons designated for fixed targets. Instead, bomber crews headed for their first pre-planned targets and then were on call to be redirected to other targets."

■ An Air Force B-52G from the 28th Air Expeditionary Wing takes off from Diego Garcia on October 22, 2001, leaving a trail of smoke above a row of B-1Bs. By that time, Air Force B-2A, B-1B, and B-52H bombers had expended more than 80 percent of the tonnage dropped on combat missions over Afghanistan. *USAF photo, Sgt. Shane Cuomo*

Grant mentions a "stunning demonstration of the new technique at its best came when a B-52 bomber put ordnance on target within 20 minutes of a call for assistance. . . . A U.S. forward air controller on the ground with the Northern Alliance forces contacted the CAOC, which passed the target to a B-52 overhead—19 minutes after the initial call the B-52 dropped its load on the enemy."

Grant also reported that at the Air Force Association symposium in Orlando, Florida, in February 2002, Air Force Chief of Staff Gen. John Jumper called the use of the B-52 against emerging targets in a close air support role "transformational," noting that these sorties, "would normally have been flown by attack aircraft such as the A-10."

By November, the Northern Alliance had captured Kabul from the Taliban, and United States forces had "boots on the ground" in Afghanistan. By December, the focus of the war was on the interception of Taliban and al-Qaeda members attempting to escape across the mountains into Pakistan. As we know with history's 20/20 hindsight, the war had now reached a critical turning point, and the American execution of this second phase of Operation Enduring Freedom left much to be desired—notably leaving the final takedown of Osama bin Laden himself in the column of unfinished business for nearly a decade.

By December 2001, with the Taliban government routed and sizable numbers of American forces arriving on the ground in Afghanistan, the nature of air operations changed. For one thing, U.S. Air Force tactical air power was now based in-country and could respond much more quickly. Bagram AB went from being an American target to being a major American base.

In March 2002, when American forces launched Operation Anaconda, their largest ground action to date, into the rugged mountains along the Pakistan border, air support included AC-130 gunships, more than three dozen tactical aircraft, and ten bombers from the 40th Air Expeditionary Wing. It has been noted that the B-52Hs from the 40th AEW flew more than eighty sorties, dropping more than half the tonnage of ordnance delivered in Operation Anaconda.

■ An enemy location in the Gardez Valley of Afghanistan is destroyed by precision munitions dropped by B-52H bombers on March 10, 2002, during Operation Anaconda. *U.S. Army photo, Specialist Andres Rodriguez*

■ A B-52H Stratofortress, flown by Capt. Will Byers and Maj. Tom Aranda, prepares for refueling over Afghanistan during a February 2006 mission. *USAF photo, Master Sgt. Lance Cheung*

■ While providing close air support for forces on the ground in Afghanistan, Maj. Andrea Jensen, a 40th Expeditionary Group B-52H pilot, accumulated one hundred combat flying hours through March 20, 2006. *USAF photo, Senior Master Sgt. John Rohrer*

■ A B-52H Stratofortress, its external racks filled with JDAMs, on its way to a combat mission over Afghanistan in May 2006. *USAF photo, Senior Master Sgt. John Rohrer*

The actions of the 40th AEW during the first five months of Operation Enduring Freedom would set the pattern of Stratofortress ground-support operations out of Diego Garcia that would be ongoing for the next five years.

A series of interviews conducted in 2006 by Master Sgt. Scott King, and posted by 40th Air Expeditionary Group Public Affairs, are illustrative of the routine for B-52 pilots forward-deployed to Diego Garcia during those years.

Maj. Andrea Jensen, with more than one hundred combat hours over Afghanistan, observed that "our task is different from day to day over Afghanistan. At times we are asked by the joint terminal attack controllers on the ground, to provide a show of force by coming in low and dropping flares. Other times, when requested, we actually drop bombs—either way, we always have successful effects against the enemy. The controllers are extremely professional at what they do. They bring a calm demeanor in the midst of chaotic conditions on the ground. Up in the air, we're pretty far removed from what's happening on the ground. I'm just happy we can assist when our forces are in harm's way."

She added that "providing close air support for our U.S. and coalition ground troops using the B-52 platform allows our ground forces to get some sleep at night."

Meanwhile, by April 2006, Lt. Col. Larry Littrell and Maj. Eric Johnson had each reached five thousand hours of flying Enduring Freedom support missions from Diego Garcia.

"To give you an idea of how hard it is to reach 5,000 hours, I have never left the cockpit of the B-52," Littrell told King. "My first Air Force assignment was to the BUFF, and I have been flying it ever since. I was flying for a commercial airline on September 11, and decided to return to active duty after the attacks on our nation. I am part of this fight. Al-Qaeda and [the] Taliban need to go away and since you can't change the way they think, you have to do it the old fashioned way. As B-52 aircrew, we have the responsibility to provide close air support for our troops on the ground. They are in harm's way every day, and for them to know that a B-52 is only minutes away, poised to support them with massive firepower, should give them a piece of mind that America hasn't forgotten them, and nothing shows resolve better than a 2,000-pound JDAM bomb. . . I think our role in Afghanistan brings the GWOT fight to their home turf instead of on the streets of Hometown USA."

As reported by *Air Force Times*, the support of Operation Enduring Freedom by the bombers from Diego Garcia formally came to an end on August 15, 2006, after four years and eleven months—one year and two months longer than the United States was embroiled in World War II.

Iraqi Freedom

In 2003, a year after Operation Anaconda and the difficult fighting in the mountains along the Afghanistan-Pakistan border, the United States launched another war in

■ B-52H navigator Capt. Michelle Gillespie of the 40th Expeditionary Bombardment Squadron checks winds over the target area during an April 2003 mission. *USAF photo, Sgt. Richard Freeland*

■ First Lieutenant Darrick Mosley, a B-52H copilot with the 40th Expeditionary Bombardment Squadron, checks flight instruments during a mission over Iraq on March 26, 2003. *USAF photo, Sgt. Richard Freeland*

Airmen prepare B-52Hs and KC-135 Stratotankers at Diego Garcia for an Operation Iraqi Freedom mission on April 9, 2003. *USAF photo, Sgt. Janice Cannon*

a different, though not unfamiliar, theater of operations. The objective of Operation Iraqi Freedom was to remove Iraqi dictator Saddam Hussein from power and to prevent his use or dissemination of chemical and biological weapons. The former objective was achieved, though it was determined after the war that he did not actually possess the latter.

Operation Iraqi Freedom had often been compared to Operation Desert Storm because it took place in the same theater against the same opponent. However, it was a much larger operation, but done with a smaller force. In the earlier conflict, the United States had been joined by a broad Coalition, but in Iraqi Freedom, the United Kingdom and Australia provided the only significant air elements to augment the American presence. The Coalition air power component for Operation Iraqi Freedom was under the control the Combined Force Air Component Commander (CFACC), U.S. Air Force Lt. Gen. Michael Moseley, who had also directed such operations in Afghanistan.

The U.S. Air Force had more than 4,900 combat aircraft (including 254 B-52s) available at the time of Desert Storm, but only around 2,000 (including 85 B-52s) at the time of Iraqi Freedom. A decade of "peace dividends" had taken a toll.

Iraqi Freedom began on the night of March 19, 2003, with an unsuccessful attempt to kill Saddam Hussein in an F-117A attack. Further air operations, combined with a ground offensive, began the following day. Though Iraq's air defenses had been somewhat degraded over the previous decade by air attacks associated with the

A 40th Expeditionary Bombardment Squadron copilot carefully guides his B-52G into position behind a KC-135 tanker on April 11, 2003.
USAF photo, Sgt. Richard Freeland

A solo B-52G from the 40th Expeditionary Bombardment Squadron flies back to Diego Garcia after striking multiple targets deep in Iraqi territory on April 7, 2003.
USAF photo, Sgt. Richard Freeland

▪ A B-52H is refueled at RAF Fairford before heading out on its next mission. During Iraqi Freedom, the base was the home of the 457th Air Expeditionary Group. *USAF photo, Airman First Class Stacia Willis*

▪ A B-52H from the 457th Air Expeditionary Group takes off from RAF Fairford for its one hundredth Iraqi Freedom combat mission on April 11, 2003. *USAF*

UN-mandated Operations Northern Watch and Southern Watch, Iraq was able to launch more than a thousand SAMs at Allied aircraft as they struck targets around Baghdad, Basra, and elsewhere.

The U.S. Air Force deployed 28 B-52Hs, including six from the Air Force Reserve Command. These aircraft were accompanied by 11 B-1Bs and four B-2As. The BUFFs included those of the 40th Air Expeditionary Wing flying from Diego Garcia, as well as a contingent of fourteen from the 457th Air Expeditionary Group, which included 23rd and 93rd Bombardment Group crews who forward-deployed to RAF Fairford in the United Kingdom on March 3 in anticipation of the operation.

Combat operations in the invasion phase of Operation Iraqi Freedom were short. On April 6, the Coalition declared air supremacy over all of the country, and Baghdad fell to the Coalition three days later. Although counterinsurgency operations would continue for years, major combat—at least by strategic air power—was essentially over within six weeks. Saddam Hussein was finally captured in December, hiding in a "spider hole" near Tikrit.

Statistically, 68 percent of the weapons dropped by the U.S. Air Force were precision-guided weapons, with over half of the latter being a total of 5,086 GBU-31 JDAMs and 7,114 GBU-12 Paveway II laser-guided bombs.

During Iraqi Freedom, some B-52Hs were equipped with the Rafael/Northrop Grumman AN/AAQ-28 Litening II targeting pod. This system incorporates magnifying day-night optics, and a high-resolution forward-looking infrared (FLIR) sensor that displays real-time images, as well as a laser designator. This allows the Stratofortress's radar-navigator to designate the targets and launch laser-guided munitions without having to depend on a forward air controller to laser designate the target. The 87-inch pod is carried on one of the aircraft's external stores pylons.

The Litening system originated in 1992 with the Rafael Advanced Defense Systems Missiles Division in Israel. In 1995, Rafael joined with Northrop Grumman to further develop Litening for the American market. The more advanced Litening II was available by 1999.

Litening II was first used by B-52H crews on the night of April 12, 2003, to launch Paveway IIs against Iraqi targets. The use of Litening II by the BUFFs had previously been controversial within the service because many felt that the system to be better suited to tactical aircraft such as the F-16, but objections have been overcome by results.

As in the war in Afghanistan, the ability of the BUFF to spend a great deal of time circling over the target made it an extremely effective ground support platform. As Capt. Patrick McDonald, a radar navigator with the 5th Bombardment Wing at Minot AFB, told Lorenzo Cortes for an article published in *Defense Daily* on May 9, 2003, "we have a very long loiter time, and, we have a very large arsenal"—an arsenal that ranges from Mk 82 500-pound bombs to the AGM-86C CALCM, both of which were used against Iraq in 2003.

=12= Back to the Future

THE MORE THINGS CHANGE, the more they remain the same. Back in the twentieth century, someone joked that the longest-running program at the United States Defense Department was the effort to find a successor for the B-52. In the twenty-first century, this program, or series of programs, is still ongoing with no end in sight.

In the 1960s, there was the XB-70, then the LAMP and AMPSS, which led to the AMSA, which led to the B-1A. In the 1980s, there was the LRCA project, which resulted in the B-1B. None ultimately resulted in a B-52 replacement.

By the twenty-first century, the U.S. Air Force was working on its Next-Generation Bomber program and its 2037 Bomber project. In both, there are discussions of replacing this aircraft we have called venerable for more than a quarter century. Meanwhile, however, the U.S. Air Force has also announced plans to keep the B-52H in service until 2045, more than ninety years after the Stratofortress first became operational.

A New Mothership

Not all of the Stratofortresses still in service at the turn of the century were B-52Hs. Even a decade after the last B-52Gs were being sent to the chopping block or to museums, one B-52B airframe still soldiered on. This aircraft, the oldest operational Stratofortress still flying, was *Balls Eight*, the ex-RB-52B redesignated as an NB-52B, the carrier aircraft that had served the U.S. Air Force and NASA as the mothership for air-launching a broad range of research aircraft from the X-15 to the X-43A.

On November 16, 2004, *Balls Eight* flew its last mission, launching the X-43A from 40,000 feet, for a test flight to 110,000 feet at a speed of around Mach 9.6. NASA's official history of the career of *Balls Eight* mentions that the aircraft's "first and last mission launched hypersonic research vehicles, the first being launch of the number one X-15 in 1960."

Balls Eight was formally retired a month later on December 17, the 101st anniversary of the first Wright Brothers flight. After forty-four years as a mothership, the aircraft remains on display at NASA's Dryden Flight Research Center at Edwards AFB, its home for all those years.

In the meantime, NASA acquired a successor aircraft—a Stratofortress, of course—a B-52H, tail number 61-0025, from the 23rd Bombardment Squadron of the 5th

Bombardment Wing at Minot AFB in North Dakota. The aircraft was officially transferred to NASA under the designation NB-52H, but it remained unused for several years after the retirement of *Balls Eight* in 2004. As mentioned in a NASA press release, "with no research projects requiring its capabilities on the horizon under NASA's restructured aeronautics research programs, the decision was made to return the [NB-52H] to the Air Force, which intends to use it as a training aid for B-52 ground technicians. Physical transfer of the aircraft is expected to occur in mid-2007."

However, by 2006, ground tests of the Boeing X-51A Waverider unmanned hypersonic scramjet research aircraft were moving forward, and the NB-52H had a renewed purpose. In December 2009, the new mothership carried the X-51A on its first captive flight, mounted on a pylon built by NASA at Dryden. In turn, the aircraft carried the Waverider for its first actual flight, which achieved a speed of Mach 5, on May 26, 2010. The NB-52H flew a second Waverider test mission on June 13, 2011.

Painted overall gloss white, NASA's NB-52H is expected to be a fixture at Dryden for as long as its fellow B-52Hs serve with the U.S. Air Force.

Continuing Upgrades

In order to keep the B-52H bomber fleet ready for the decades ahead, the early twenty-first century was marked by upgrades, including the Avionics Midlife Improvement (AMI) program. Specifics include the AN/ARC-210 VHF/UHF and AN/ARC-310

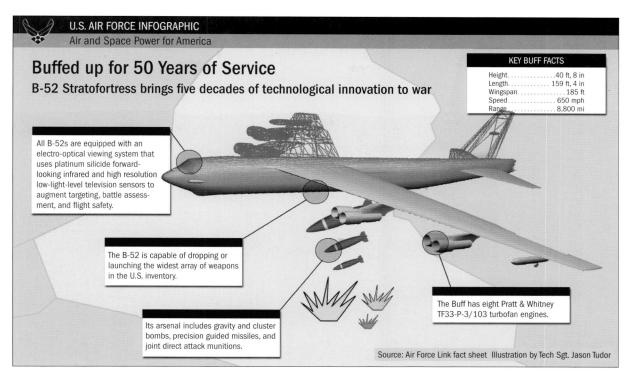

U.S. AIR FORCE INFOGRAPHIC
Air and Space Power for America

Buffed up for 50 Years of Service

B-52 Stratofortress brings five decades of technological innovation to war

KEY BUFF FACTS

Height	40 ft, 8 in
Length	159 ft, 4 in
Wingspan	185 ft
Speed	650 mph
Range	8,800 mi

All B-52s are equipped with an electro-optical viewing system that uses platinum silicide forward-looking infrared and high resolution low-light-level television sensors to augment targeting, battle assessment, and flight safety.

The B-52 is capable of dropping or launching the widest array of weapons in the U.S. inventory.

The Buff has eight Pratt & Whitney TF33-P-3/103 turbofan engines.

Its arsenal includes gravity and cluster bombs, precision guided missiles, and joint direct attack munitions.

Source: Air Force Link fact sheet Illustration by Tech Sgt. Jason Tudor

high-frequency communications systems. These were subsequently upgraded to NATO Demand Assigned Multiple Access (DAMA) standard, allowing channels to be used by multiple users sequentially and greatly increasing the pool of circuits over a Permanently Assigned Multiple Access (PAMA) system.

Electronic systems upgrades undertaken around the turn of the century included the Harpoon Aircraft Command Launch Control Set (HACLCS), which had been installed in the B-52G in the 1980s, but not in the B-52H until it was adapted to operate with the AGM-84 Harpoon and AGM-84E SLAM. It was subsequently superseded by the Harpoon Stores Management Overlay (SMO).

Ongoing at the time of Operations Enduring Freedom and Iraqi Freedom was the B-52H Situational Awareness Defensive Improvement (SADI) program, under which Lockheed Martin was studying the replacement of the Rivet Ace–era ALR-20A wideband countermeasures receiver and the AN/ALR-46 digital radar warning receiver.

It is a testament to the importance which the B-52H still holds for the U.S. Air Force that many details of the upgrades are still cloaked in secrecy.

Discussions of numerous potential changes continue to be ongoing. One of the major Stratofortress upgrades which has been deliberated on and off since the 1970s has been re-engining. The idea is, essentially, to retrofit the Stratofortress with high-bypass turbofan engines of the type used on modern jetliners such as Boeing's 747 or 767. Representing newer-generation technology that is now well-established in the airline industry worldwide, these would be much more efficient than the J57 turbojets of the early Stratofortresses or the TF33 turbofans of the B-52H.

An official graphic illustrating twenty-first century upgrades to the B-52H. *USAF*

The Air Force Flight Test Center NB-52H from Edwards AFB, California, carries the X-51A WaveRider prior to the scramjet's first hypersonic flight test on March 26, 2010. *USAF*

A B-52H Stratofortresses taxis to its parking spot at Andersen AFB after landing in February 2004. BUFFs from Minot AFB were deploying to this base to support U.S. Pacific Command's request for a rotational bomber force on Guam. *USAF photo, Sgt. Bennie Davis III*

In 1996, Boeing, along with Rolls-Royce, Allison, and American Airlines, submitted an unsolicited proposal to re-engine B-52Hs with four 43,100-pound thrust RB-211-535E4-B turbofans. One each would have replaced each pair of TF33s on the same engine pylons. The resulting aircraft might have been redesignated as "B-52J." The proposal showed that the new turbofans would increase power and range, while greatly reducing the cost of operation, but the U.S. Air Force declined.

Stephen Trimble reported in *Aviation Week* in July 2003, that the service was back for another look, this time replacing eight engines with eight, rather than four, high-bypass turbofans.

This proposal was in turn, followed by other studies. Among these was the Task Force on B-52H Re-engining, empaneled in 2004 by Michael Wynne, the Undersecretary for Defense Acquisition, Technology, and Logistics (later Secretary of the Air Force). A year later, the Air Force Agile Combat Support Systems Wing and the Propulsion Systems Squadron at Wright-Patterson AFB undertook the *B-52 Propulsion Capability Study*. Though fuel cost savings and improved performance were clearly demonstrated, neither project led to the Defense Department being willing or able to fund the cost of such an ambitious undertaking. Additional studies have been, and will continue to be, commissioned.

B-52s in the U.S. Air Force Inventory: Post—Cold War Era

A row of B-52H Stratofortresses from Barksdale AFB and Minot AFB await their next mission, on the flight line at Andersen AFB in February 2007. The different colored tail markings represent the individual squadrons to which each bomber was assigned. *USAF photo, Senior Master Sgt. Don Perrien*

	Total	TAI	PAI	Avgerage Age	Air Force Reserve		Total	TAI	PAI	Avgerage Age	Air Force Reserve
1992	148	148	159	31.4	0	2002	84	84	49	40.8	9
1993	136	136	118	32.2	2	2003	85	67	52	41.8	9
1994	85	84	82	32.8	9	2004	84	84	53	42.8	9
1995	85	85	67	33.8	9	2005	85	85	54	43.8	9
1996	85	85	49	34.8	9	2006	85	67	51	44.8	9
1997	85	85	49	35.8	9	2007	85	85	54	45.8	9
1998	85	85	49	36.8	9	2008	67	66	51	46.8	9
1999	85	73	59	37.8	9	2009	68	68	45	47.8	9
2000	85	85	49	38.8	9	2010	74	*	*	48.8	9
2001	85	85	49	39.8	9						

Note: The 1992–1993 period marked the retirement of the B-52G fleet.

TAI: Total Active Inventory—aircraft assigned to operating forces for mission, training, test, or maintenance. Includes primary, backup, and attrition reserve aircraft.

PAI: Primary Aircraft Inventory—aircraft assigned to meet Primary Aircraft Authorization (PAA).

* TAI and PAI data no longer listed.

Source: Air Force Almanac

■ A B-52H from the 23rd Expeditionary Bombardment Squadron stabilizes during air refueling near Andersen AFB, Guam. *USAF photo, Sgt. Patrick Mitchell*

Many years after any other aircraft would have been turned out to pasture at Davis-Monthan, the Air Force was still thinking up new duties for the BUFF. In the first decade of the new century, there was a great deal of discussion about adapting it as a radar jamming platform under the designation EB-52H. As Michael Sirak wrote in *Jane's Defence Weekly*, on December 11, 2002, "the Air Force wants to equip its B-52H Stratofortress bombers with the capability to jam enemy air defenses. . . The U.S. Air Force is defining the requirements

The venerable BUFF's twenty-first century flight deck: A B-52H Stratofortress crew prepares to take fuel from a KC-135 Stratotanker during a training mission. USAF

Left: A B-52H Stratofortress takes on fuel from a KC-135 Stratotanker over the Pacific during Exercise Cope North on February 22, 2011. *USAF photo, Sgt. Angelita Lawrence* ▪ Right: A 20th Bombardment Squadron B-52H flies over the Pacific Ocean after an air refueling during the Rim of the Pacific (RIMPAC) exercise in July 2010. RIMPAC is a biennial multinational exercise designed to strengthen regional partnerships and improve interoperability. *USAF photo, Sgt. Kamaile Long*

B-52H Selected Weapons Systems Options

Sgt. Joshua Cormier and Senior Airman Merritt Shaw perform phase maintenance on a B-52H inside Hangar 1 at Andersen AFB in January 2006. *USAF photo, Sgt. Shane Cuomo*

NUCLEAR WEAPONS

20 Boeing AGM86B AirLaunched Cruise Missiles (ALCM)

(12 on two underwing pylons; 8 on an internal rotary launcher)

12 Raytheon AGM129 Advanced Cruise Missiles (ACM)
    (on two underwing pylons; retired after 2007)

2 B53 thermonuclear bombs (within the bomb bay; retired after 1997)

8 B61 thermonuclear bombs (within the bomb bay)

8 B83 thermonuclear bombs (within the bomb bay)

CONVENTIONAL PRECISION/GUIDED WEAPONS

20 Boeing AGM86C Conventional AirLaunched
    Cruise Missiles (CALCM)

(12 on two underwing pylons; 8 on an internal
    rotary launcher)

18 Joint Direct Attack Munition (JDAM)
    (12 on two underwing pylons)

8 Boeing AGM-84 Harpoon

8 Rafael/Lockheed Martin AGM-142 Popeye (Have Nap)

18 Raytheon AGM154 Joint Standoff Weapon (JSOW)
    (12 on two underwing pylons)

12 Lockheed Martin AGM158 Joint AirtoSurface Standoff
    Missile (JASSM) (on two underwing pylons)

30 Wind Corrected Munitions Dispenser (WCMD)
    (16 on two underwing pylons)

CONVENTIONAL GRAVITY WEAPONS

51 Mk 36 500-pound DST Destructor Mine

8 Mk 41 2,000-pound DST Destructor Mine

12 Mk 52 1000-pound aircraftlaid bottom mine

8 Mk 55 1000-pound aircraftlaid bottom mine

8 Mk 56 2000-pound antisubmarine mine

8 Mk 60 Alliant Techsystems 2,370-pound
Encapsulated Torpedo (CAPTOR)

51 Mk 62 500-pound Quick Strike Mine

8 Mk 64 2,000-pound Quick Strike Mine

8 Mk 65 2,000-pound Quick Strike Mine

51 Mk 82 500-pound General Purpose Bomb

18 Mk 84 2,000-pound General Purpose Bomb
    (on two underwing pylons)

51 M117 750-pound General Purpose Bomb

CONVENTIONAL GRAVITY WEAPONS
   (CLUSTER BOMB UNITS)

51 CBU-52 70-pound antipersonnel weapon
    (27 within the bomb bay, 18 on two underwing pylons)

51 CBU-58 800-pound incendiary weapon
    (27 within the bomb bay, 18 on two underwing pylons)

51 CBU-71 incendiary weapon
    (27 within the bomb bay, 18 on two underwing pylons)

30 CBU-87 1,000-pound, Combined Effects Munition (CEM)
    (6 within the bomb bay, 18 on two underwing pylons)

30 CBU-89 1,000-pound Gator Mine
    (6 within the bomb bay, 18 on two underwing pylons)

30 CBU-97 1,000-pound sensorfused antiarmor weapon
    (6 within the bomb bay, 18 on two underwing pylons)

Note: Not all are carried simultaneously.

Performing a preflight check aboard a B-52H in April 2011 at Minot AFB, in preparation for an eight-hour training mission. *USAF photo, Sgt. Andy Kin*

The weapons carried by the B-52H Stratofortress are seen here on static display at Barksdale AFB in Louisiana in 2006. Note the rotary launcher with AGM-86 Air-Launched Cruise Missiles in the center. *USAF photo, Sgt. Robert Horstman*

for the airborne electronic attack (AEA) variant of the bomber, which it notionally calls the EB-52H. The aircraft could suppress enemy air-defence capabilities while operating safely outside their range (stand-off jamming), or could lead a strike package over hostile territory (stand-in), and remain there for long periods (stand-on), according to officials in the U.S. Air Force's Air Combat Command (ACC)."

Terry Bott, the deputy chief of the B-52 Weapon System Team in the Air Combat Command's directorate of requirements, told Sirak that "we think the B-52 is great for this [role]. Not only that, we can also bring in the electronic-warfare capability, and right along with it, a very large load of weapons" to attack the air defenses and targets of opportunity that may emerge."

The shortfall in jamming capacity existed in the U.S. Air Force arsenal following the retirement of the General Dynamics/Grumman EF-111A Raven in 1998. Those who chart the course of how the BUFF outlived younger aircraft will note that the EF-111A was the last variant of the F-111 family, which entered service nearly two decades after the Stratofortress and included the FB-111, which served along side the B-52 in the SAC arsenal for many years.

Under the B-52 Stand-Off Jammer (SOJ) program, work began in 2002 on developing jamming pods for the EB-52H aircraft. Having spoken with Lt. Col. Scott Hardiman,

The Air Force Global Strike Command (AFGSC) was activated in 2009, receiving the nuclear-capable assets of the Air Force Space Command on December 1, 2009, and the nuclear-capable assets of the Air Combat Command on February 1, 2010. *USAF*

commander of the Airborne Electronic Attack Systems Squadron at Wright-Patterson AFB, Marc Selinger wrote in *Aviation Week* in September 2005, "the Air Force has indicated that it hopes to achieve a full operational capability with SOJ in fiscal 2012-FY '15."

However, the SOJ was cancelled in a high-level review later in 2005, only to be revived later, and cancelled again in 2009. The service decided to rely on Unmanned Aerial Vehicles, and assistance from the U.S. Navy's EF-18G Growler.

B-52H Selected Electronics Systems

■ Capt. Jeremiah Baldwin (left), pilot, and Lt. Bentley Brooks, copilot, conduct a preflight check in their 23rd Bombardment Squadron B-52H at Andersen AFB in March 2004. *USAF photo, Master Sgt. Val Gempis*

AN/AAQ6 FLIR Electrooptical viewing system
AN/ALE20 Infrared flare dispensers (12)
AN/ALE24 Chaff dispensers (6)
AN/ALQ117 Pave Mint active countermeasures set
AN/ALQ122 Motorola false target generator
AN/ALQ153 Northrop Grumman tail warning set
AN/ALQ155 Northrop Grumman jammer Power Management System
AN/ALQ172(V)2 ITT electronic countermeasures system
AN/ALR20A Wideband countermeasures radar warning receiver
AN/ALR46 Litton digital warning receiver
AN/ALT32 Noise jammer

AN/ANS136 Inertial Navigation Set
AN/APN224 Radar Altimeter
AN/APQ156 Strategic Radar
AN/ARC210 VHF/UHF communications
AN/ARC310 HF radio communications
AN/ASN134 Heading Reference
AN/ASQ175 Control Display Set
AN/AVQ22 Lowlight TV Electrooptical viewing system
AN/AYK17 Digital Data Display
AN/AYQ10 Ballistics Computer

During the early twenty-first century, the arsenal carried by the BUFF continued to evolve. Based on the operational experience gained during Enduring Freedom and Iraqi Freedom, the Air Force sought to upgrade the targeting capability of the JDAM by adding a precision laser terminal guidance seeker to the JDAM kit. The resulting Laser JDAM (LJDAM) kit incorporates a DSU-38/B laser seeker with a Precision Laser Guidance Set (PLGS) to provide the capability of hitting moving targets. In 2007, Boeing received a contract for 600 LJDAMs, which were originally intended to equip F-15Es and F-16s. They were first demonstrated as part of the arsenal of the B-52H in September 2008.

As noted in Chapter 10, it was also in 2007 that the U.S. Air Force announced plans to phase out its entire inventory of stealthy AGM-129 Advanced Cruise Missiles because of maintenance costs. The older AGM-86B ALCM and AGM-86C CALCM cruise missiles would be retained indefinitely. At that time, the service had 460 AGM-129s, and 1,140 of the older missiles, though the number was gradually being reduced.

In the process of decommissioning the AGM-129s, the Air Force experienced an unexpected incident that altered its history. On the night of August 29, a B-52H took off from Minot AFB carrying six AGM-129s bound for Barksdale AFB for decommissioning. It was a routine flight, one of many, in which the W80-1 thermonuclear warheads

■ In this dramatic image, airmen from the 5th Aircraft Maintenance Squadron at Minot AFB in North Dakota conduct a fuel enrichment valve test on a B-52H in mid-January as the temperature sits at six below zero, Fahrenheit. Crews were modifying fuel controls for cold-weather engine start-ups. *USAF photo, Airman Fallon Shea*

A B-52H from the 20th Expeditionary Bomb Squadron over the Pacific Ocean during the RIMPAC exercise in July 2010. *USAF photo, Sgt. Jacob Bailey*

Capt. Jeff Rogers (left) and Lt. Patrick Applegate in the lower deck of a 5th Bombardment Wing B-52H at Minot AFB in August 2006. *USAF photo, Master Sgt. Lance Cheung*

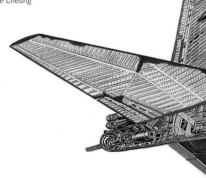

NUCLEAR WEAPONS:

B83

B61

A B-52H aircrew assigned to the 96th Bombardment Squadron at Barksdale AFB flies a Red Flag Alaska mission from Eielson AFB on April 29, 2010. *USAF photo, Sgt. Christopher Boitz*

B-52H Stratofortress

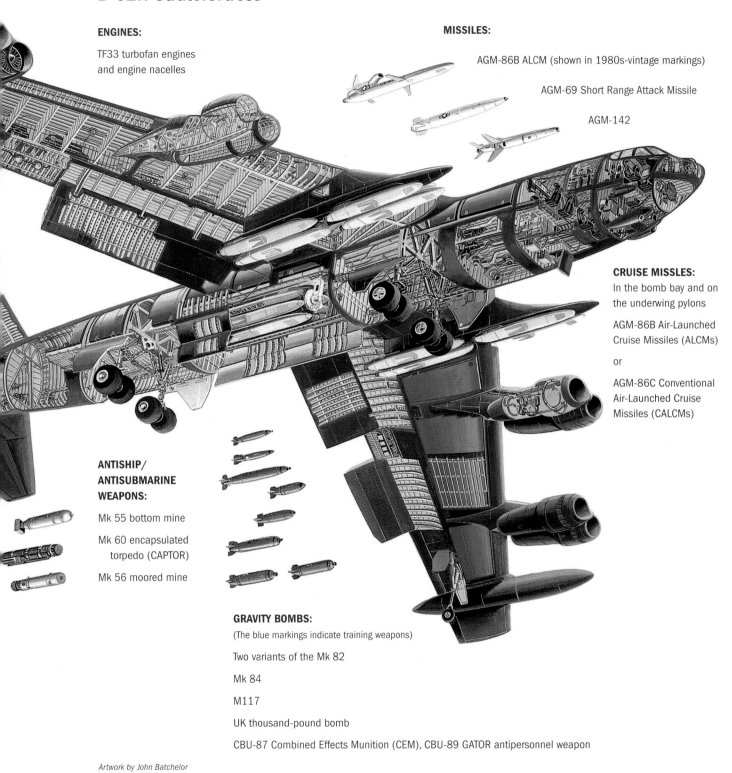

ENGINES:

TF33 turbofan engines and engine nacelles

MISSILES:

AGM-86B ALCM (shown in 1980s-vintage markings)

AGM-69 Short Range Attack Missile

AGM-142

CRUISE MISSLES:

In the bomb bay and on the underwing pylons

AGM-86B Air-Launched Cruise Missiles (ALCMs)

or

AGM-86C Conventional Air-Launched Cruise Missiles (CALCMs)

ANTISHIP/ ANTISUBMARINE WEAPONS:

Mk 55 bottom mine

Mk 60 encapsulated torpedo (CAPTOR)

Mk 56 moored mine

GRAVITY BOMBS:

(The blue markings indicate training weapons)

Two variants of the Mk 82

Mk 84

M117

UK thousand-pound bomb

CBU-87 Combined Effects Munition (CEM), CBU-89 GATOR antipersonnel weapon

Artwork by John Batchelor

A B-52H Stratofortress is "intercepted" by two U.S. Navy F/A-18 Hornets as it flies past the USS *Nimitz* in May 2008. The BUFF was from the 96th Expeditionary Bombardment Squadron deployed to Andersen AFB, Guam. *U.S. Navy*

were supposed to have been removed from the missiles—but that night, they had *not* been. The armed missiles arrived safely, but the fact that the error was not discovered for thirty-six hours, at *either base*, underscored a serious lapse of oversight.

"Air Force standards are very exacting when it comes to munitions handling," spokesman Lt. Col. Ed Thomas said in an official statement. "The weapons were always in our custody and there was never a danger to the American public."

There was considerable fallout from the incident, but fortunately it was political, not radioactive.

Heads rolled. Beginning with the 5th Bombardment Wing commander at Minot and the 2nd Operations Group commander at Barksdale, more than five dozen Air Force personnel were relieved of command or lost their certification in the personnel reliability program. After a series of investigations by the U.S. Air Force and the Defense Science Board, the top Air Force leadership, Secretary of the Air Force Michael Wynne and Chief of Staff Gen. Michael Moseley were asked to resign.

For the Air Force going forward, the biggest change wrought by the incident was that nuclear weapons capability was withdrawn from Air Combat Command, who had managed bombers since 1992, and from Air Force Space Command, which managed ICBMs, and placed in a newly created organization. The Air Force Global Strike Command (AFGSC), which became operational on August 7, 2009, had a mission that made it seem a great deal like the Strategic Air Command of old.

In early 2005, the U.S. Air Force awarded Boeing a multiyear contract to upgrade B-52 communications under the Combat Network Communications Technology (CONECT) program. As Marc Selinger wrote in *Aviation Week*, the contract called for

"integrating new satellite communications and other enhancements into the B-52 to improve its ability to share information with other aircraft and with command centers. . . . The modifications also will enable the bomber to retarget its weapons after it has taken off. The Air Force plans to put all 76 active B-52s through the CONECT program. Up to 18 reserve aircraft may be modified as well."

In a July 12, 2005, article, Selinger reported that, as part of the CONECT program, the Air Force planned to "replace old analog displays in the cockpit with new color displays. . . . [and] equip the early-1960s bomber for 21st-century information-sharing and situational awareness."

The first successful flight of a CONECT-modified B-52H was launched from Edwards AFB on January 17, 2010, and on August 3, 2011, the aircraft's crew successfully completed an evaluation flight of the CONECT interphone system. According to Scot Oathout, Boeing's B-52 program director, the system demonstrated that CONECT had given the B-52H "the ability to participate in net-centric operations. This means the aircraft can exchange real-time digital information with other ground-based and airborne assets while on a mission, increasing its effectiveness, survivability and lethality. CONECT keeps the B-52 in the fight."

And so it goes. The duration of the BUFF's career long ago surpassed the life span of those who created it and the careers of those who first flew it. It has flown long after the end of the careers of those who first flew it in combat, and it will continue to fly and fight beyond the span of the careers of those who flew it over the mountains of Afghanistan.

It will be nearly halfway through the twenty-first century before any book of the type you now hold can end with a phrase other than "to be continued."

Reassigned from Air Combat Command to the Air Force Global Strike Command in February 2010, a B-52H Stratofortress and a B-2A Spirit make a formation flight. *USAF*

Appendix 1

Specifications by Stratofortress Model

XB-52 (Boeing Model 464-67)

Length: 152 feet 8 inches

Wingspan: 185 feet

Tail height: 48 feet 3.6 inches

Wing area: 4,000 square feet

Weight: 155,200 pounds empty;
390,000 pounds gross

Maximum speed: 611 mph at 20,000 feet;
594 mph at 35,000 feet

Cruising speed: 519 mph

Service ceiling: 46,500 feet

Combat radius: 3,535 miles with 10,000
pound bomb load

Ferry range: 7,015 miles

Powerplant:
Eight Pratt & Whitney YJ57-P-3 turbojets
(8,700 pounds of thrust each)

YB-52 (Boeing Model 464-67)

Length: 152 feet 8 inches

Wingspan: 185 feet

Tail height: 48 feet 3.6 inches

Wing area: 4,000 square feet

Weight: 155,200 pounds empty; 405,000
pounds gross

Maximum speed: 611 mph at 20,000 feet;
594 mph at 35,000 feet

Cruising speed: 519 mph

Service ceiling: 46,500 feet

Combat radius: 3,545 miles with 10,000 pound
bomb load

Ferry range: 7,015 miles

Powerplant: Eight Pratt & Whitney YJ57-P-3
turbojets (8,700 pounds of thrust each)

B-52A (Boeing Model 464-201-0)

Length: 156 feet 6.9 inches

Wingspan: 185 feet

Tail height: 48 feet 3.6 inches

Wing area: 4,000 square feet

Weight: 420,000 pounds gross

Armament: Four .50-caliber M3 machine guns with 600 rounds in tail turret

Maximum offensive payload: 43,000 pounds

Service ceiling: 46,500 feet

Combat radius: 3,590 miles

Powerplant: Eight Pratt & Whitney J57-P-1W turbojets (10,000 pounds of thrust dry, and 11,000 pounds of thrust with water injection)

B-52B/RB-52B (Boeing Model 464-201-4/464-201-3)

Length: 156 feet 6.9 inches

Wingspan: 185 feet

Tail height: 48 feet 3.6 inches

Wing area: 4,000 square feet

Weight: 164,081 pounds empty; 272,000 pounds combat; 420,000 pounds gross

Armament: Two 20mm M24A1 cannons with 400 rounds, or four .50-caliber M3 machine guns with 600 rounds in tail turret

Maximum offensive payload: 43,000 pounds

Maximum speed: 630 mph at 19,800 feet; 598 mph at 35,000 feet; 571 mph at 45,750 feet

Cruising speed: 523 mph

Service ceiling at combat weight 47,300 feet

Combat radius: 3,590 miles with 10,000 pound bomb load

Ferry range: 7,343 miles

Powerplant: Eight Pratt & Whitney J57-P-1W, -1WA, or -1WB turbojets (11,400 pounds of thrust with water injection),

Subsequently: Eight Pratt & Whitney J57-P-29W or -29WA turbojets (10,500 pounds of thrust dry, and 12,100 pounds of thrust with water injection)

Or: Eight Pratt & Whitney J57-P-19W turbojets (10,500 pounds of thrust dry, and 12,100 pounds of thrust with water injection)

B-52C (Boeing Model 464-201-6)

Length: 156 feet 6.9 inches

Wingspan: 185 feet

Tail height: 48 feet 3.6 inches

Wing area: 4,000 square feet

Weight: 164,486 pounds empty; 293,100 pounds combat; 450,000 pounds gross

Armament: Four .50-caliber M3 machine guns with 600 rounds in tail turret.

Maximum offensive payload: 43,000 pounds

Maximum speed: 636 mph at 20,200 feet; 570 mph at 45,000 feet

Cruising speed: 521 mph

Service ceiling at combat weight: 45,800 feet

Combat radius: 3,475 miles with 10,000 pound bomb load

Ferry range: 7,856 miles

Powerplant: Eight Pratt & Whitney J57-P-29WA or -19W turbojets (12,100 pounds of thrust with water injection)

B-52D (Boeing Model 464-201-7)

Length: 156 feet 6.9 inches

Wingspan: 185 feet

Tail height: 48 feet 3.6 inches

Wing area: 4,000 square feet

Weight: 177,816 pounds empty; 293,100 pounds combat; 450,000 pounds gross.

Armament: Four .50-caliber M3 machine guns with 600 rounds in tail turret.

Maximum offensive payload: 43,000 pounds; 60,000 (including external pylons) after "Big Belly" modifications

Maximum speed: 585 mph at 20,200 feet; 570 mph at 45,000 feet

Cruising speed: 521 mph

Service ceiling: 46,350 feet

Service ceiling at combat weight: 45,800 feet

Combat radius: 3,470 miles with 10,000 pound bomb load

Ferry range: 7,850 miles

Powerplant: Eight Pratt & Whitney J57-P-19W turbojets (12,100 pounds of thrust with water injection)

B-52E (Boeing Model 464-259)

Length: 156 feet 6.9 inches

Wingspan: 185 feet

Tail height: 48 feet 3.6 inches

Wing area: 4,000 square feet

Weight: 174,782 pounds empty; 292,460 pounds combat; 450,000 pounds gross

Armament: Four .50-caliber M3 machine guns with 600 rounds in tail turret

Maximum offensive payload: 43,000 pounds

Maximum speed: 630 mph at 19,800 feet; 570 mph at 45,050 feet

Cruising speed: 523 mph

Service ceiling at combat weight: 46,200 feet

Combat radius: 3,500 miles with 10,000 pound bomb load

Ferry range: 7,875 miles

Powerplant: Eight Pratt & Whitney J57-P-29WA or -19W turbojets (10,500 pounds of thrust dry, and 12,100 pounds of thrust with water injection)

B-52F (Boeing Model 464-260)

Length: 156 feet 6.9 inches

Wingspan: 185 feet

Tail height: 48 feet 3.6 inches

Wing area: 4,000 square feet

Weight: 173,599 pounds empty; 291,570 pounds combat; 450,000 pounds gross.

Armament: Four .50-caliber M3 machine guns with 600 rounds in tail turret.

Maximum offensive payload: 43,000 pounds

Maximum speed: 638 mph at 21,000 feet; 570 mph at 46,500 feet

Cruising speed: 523 mph

Service ceiling at combat weight: 46,700 feet

Combat radius: 3,650 miles with 10,000 pound bomb load

Ferry range: 7,976 miles

Powerplant: Eight Pratt & Whitney J57-P-43WA turbojets (11,200 pounds of thrust dry, and 13,750 pounds of thrust with water injection)

B-52G (Boeing Model 464-253)

Length: 157 feet 7 inches (later increased to 160 feet 10.9 inches)

Wingspan: 185 feet

Tail height: 40 feet 8 inches

Wing area: 4,000 square feet

Weight: 168,445 pounds empty; 302,634 pounds combat; 488,000 pounds gross

Armament: Four .50-caliber M3 machine guns with 600 rounds in tail turret.

Maximum offensive payload: 50,000 pounds

Maximum speed: 636 mph at 20,800 feet; 570 mph at 46,000 feet

Cruising speed: 523 mph

Service ceiling at combat weight: 47,000 feet

Combat radius: 4,100 miles with 10,000 pound bomb load

Ferry range: 8,900 miles (Record flight, 10,078.8 miles)

Powerplant: Eight Pratt & Whitney J57-P-43WB turbojets (13,750 pounds of thrust with water injection)

B-52H (Boeing Model 464-261)

Length: 156 feet

Wingspan: 185 feet

Tail height: 40 feet 8 inches

Wing area: 4,000 square feet

Weight: 172,740 pounds empty; 306,358 pounds combat; 488,000 pounds gross

Armament: One 20-mm M61 cannon with 1,242 rounds in tail turret

Maximum offensive payload: 50,000 pounds

Maximum speed: 632 mph at 23,800 feet; 603 mph at 35,000 feet; 560 mph at 46,650 feet

Cruising speed: 525 mph

Service ceiling at combat weight: 47,700 feet

Combat radius: 4,825 miles with 10,000 pound bomb load

Ferry range: 10,145 miles (Record flight, 12,532.28 miles)

Powerplant: Eight Pratt & Whitney TF33-P-3 turbofans (17,000 pounds of thrust each)

Appendix 2

Stratofortress Production by Model and Block Number

XB-52 (Boeing Model 464-67)
1 built in Seattle:
49-230 (XB-52-BO) c/n 16248

YB-52 (Boeing Model 464-67)
1 built in Seattle:
49-231 (YB-52-BO) c/n 16249

B-52A (Boeing Model 464-201-0)
3 built in Seattle:
52-001 through 003 (B-52A-1-BO) c/n 16491 through 16493

B-52B (Boeing Model 464-201-4)
23 built in Seattle, in 3 blocks:
53-373 through 376 (B-52B-25-BO) c/n 16852 through 16855
53-380 through 387 (B-52B-30-BO) c/n 16859 through 16866
53-388 through 398 (B-52B-35-BO) c/n 16867 through 16877

RB-52B (Boeing Model 464-201-3)
27 built in Seattle, 6 in blocks:
52-004 through 006 (RB-52B-5-BO) c/n 16494 through 16496
52-007 through 013 (RB-52B-10-BO) c/n 16497 through 16503
52-8710 through 715 (RB-52B-15-BO) c/n 16838 through 16843
52-8716 (RB-52B-20-BO) c/n 16844
53-366 through 372 (RB-52B-25-BO) c/n 16845 through 16851
53-377 through 379 (RB-52B-30-BO) c/n 16856 through 16858

B-52C (Boeing Model 464-201-6)
35 built in Seattle, in 3 blocks:
53-0399 through 0408 (B-52C-40-BO) c/n 16878 through 16887
54-2664 through 2675 (B-52C-45-BO) c/n 17159 through 17170
54-2676 through 2688 (B-52C-50-BO) c/n 17171 through 17183

B-52D (Boeing Model 464-201-7)

69 built in Wichita, in 10 blocks:

55-0049 through 0051 (B-52D-1-BW) c/n 464001 through 464003
55-0052 through 0054 (B-52D-5-BW) c/n 464004 through 046006
55-0055 through 0060 (B-52D-10-BW) c/n 464007 through 464012
55-0061 through 0064 (B-52D-15-BW) c/n 464013 through 464016
55-0065 through 0067 (B-52D-20-BW) c/n 464017 through 464019
55-0673 through 0675 (B-52D-20-BW) c/n 464020 through 464022
55-0676 through 0680 (B-52D-25-BW) c/n 464023 through 464027
56-0657 through 0668 (B-52D-30-BW) c/n 464028 through 464039
56-0669 through 0680 (B-52D-35-BW) c/n 464040 through 464051
56-0681 through 0698 (B-52D-40-BW) c/n 464052 through 464069

101 built in Seattle, in 6 blocks:

55-0068 through 0088 (B-52D-55-BO) c/n 17184 through 17204
55-0089 through 0104 (B-52D-60-BO) c/n 17205 through 17220
55-0105 through 0117 (B-52D-65-BO) c/n 17221 through 17233
56-0580 through 0590 (B-52D-70-BO) c/n 17263 through 17273
56-0591 through 0610 (B-52D-75-BO) c/n 17274 through 17293
56-0611 through 0630 (B-52D-80-BO) c/n 17294 through 17313

B-52E 59 (Boeing Model 464-259)

58 built in Wichita, in 4 blocks:

56-0699 through 0712 (B-52E-45-BW) c/n 464070 through 464083
57-0095 through 0109 (B-52E-50-BW) c/n 464084 through 464098
57-0110 through 0130 (B-52E-55-BW) c/n 464099 through 464119
57-0131 through 0138 (B-52E-60-BW) c/n 464120 through 464127

42 built in Seattle, in 4 blocks:

56-0631 through 0649 (B-52E-85-BO) c/n 17314 through 17332
56-0650 through 0656 (B-52E-90-BO) c/n 17333 through 17339
57-0014 through 0022 (B-52E-90-BO) c/n 17408 through 17416
57-0023 through 0029 (B-52E-95-BO) c/n 17417 through 17423

B-52F (Boeing Model 464-260)

45 built in Wichita, in 2 blocks:

57-139 through 154 (B-52F-65-BW) c/n 464128 through 464143
57-155 through 183 (B-52F-70-BW) c/n 464144 through 464172
57-184 through 228 (B-52F-BW) (Cancelled)

44 built in Seattle, in 3 blocks:

57-030 through 037 (B-52F-100-BO) c/n 17424 through 17431
57-038 through 052 (B-52F-105-BO) c/n 17432 through 17446
57-053 through 073 (B-52F-110-BO) c/n 17447 through 17467
57-074 through 094 (B-52F-BO) (Cancelled)

B-52G (Boeing Model 464-253)

193 built in Wichita, in 12 blocks:

57-6468 through 6475 (B-52G-75-BW) c/n 464173 through 464180
57-6476 through 6485 (B-52G-80-BW) c/n 464181 through 464190
57-6486 through 6499 (B-52G-85-BW) c/n 464191 through 464204
57-6500 through 6520 (B-52G-90-BW) c/n 464205 through 464225
58-0158 through 0187 (B-52G-95-BW) c/n 464226 through 464255
58-0188 through 0211 (B-52G-100-BW) c/n 4642256 through 464279
58-0212 through 0232 (B-52G-105-BW) c/n 464280 through 464300
58-0233 through 0246 (B-52G-110-BW) c/n 464301 through 464314
58-0247 through 0258 (B-52G-115-BW) c/n 464315 through 464326
59-2564 through 2575 (B-52G-120-BW) c/n 464327 through 464338
59-2576 through 2587 (B-52G-125-BW) c/n 464339 through 464350
59-2588 through 2602 (B-52G-130-BW) c/n 464351 through 464365
(Note: Some sources list 59-2564 through 59-2602 as all being part of Block 120.)

B-52H (Boeing Model 464-261)

102 built in Wichita, in 9 blocks:

60-0001 through 0013 (B-52H-135-BW) c/n 464366 through 464378
60-0014 through 0021 (B-52H-140-BW) c/n 464379 through 464386
60-0022 through 0033 (B-52H-145-BW) c/n 464387 through 464398
60-0034 through 0045 (B-52H-150-BW) c/n 464399 through 464410
60-0046 through 0057 (B-52H-155-BW) c/n 464411 through 464422
60-0058 through 0062 (B-52H-160-BW) c/n 464423 through 464427
61-0001 through 0013 (B-52H-165-BW) c/n 464428 through 464440
61-0014 through 0026 (B-52H-170-BW) c/n 464441 through 464453
61-0027 through 0040 (B-52H-175-BW) c/n 464454 through 464467

B-52J

0 (to date)

The designation may be applied to B-52Hs retrofitted with high-bypass turbofan engines.

Selected Modifications Resulting in Redesignations

EB-52H (designation provisionally considered for an ECM aircraft)
JB-52B (one aircraft, 52-0004, formerly RB-52B)
JB-52C (two aircraft, 53-0399 and 54-2676, formerly B-52C)
JB-52G (several aircraft temporarily redesignated, including 57-6470, 57-6473, 57-6477, 58-0159, 58-0182, formerly B-52G)
JB-52H (several aircraft temporarily redesignated, including 60-0003, 60-0004, 60-0005, 60-0023, formerly B-52H)
NB-52A (one aircraft, 52-0003, formerly B-52A)
NB-52B (one aircraft, 52-0008, formerly B-52B)
NB-52E (one aircraft, 56-0631, formerly B-52E)
NB-52H (one aircraft, 61-0025, formerly B-52H)

Stratofortress Combat Wings and Assigned Squadrons (1955–Present)

Notes:

(1) At press time, the three active, permanent Stratofortress wings in the U.S. Air Force were the 2nd Bombardment Wing at Barksdale AFB, Louisiana (tail code LA); the 5th Bombardment Wing at Minot AFB, North Dakota (tail code MT); and the 307th Bombardment Wing (Air Force Reserve Command) at Barksdale AFB, Louisiana (tail code BD).

(2) In 1960–1961, in order to disburse the Stratofortress fleet as broadly as possible for fear of enemy air attack, the SAC established a large number of provisional strategic wings designated with four-digit numbers beginning with 4. These were deactivated on February 1, 1963, and their aircraft reassigned to other units as noted below.

2nd Bombardment Wing (Heavy)

(Superseded 4238th Strategic Wing)

Barksdale AFB, Louisiana

B-52F, 1963–1965; B-52G, 1965–1992; B-52H, 1992–present

11th Bombardment Squadron (B-52H)

20th Bombardment Squadron (B-52F/H)

62nd Bombardment Squadron (B-52G)

96th Bombardment Squadron (B-52H)

596th Bombardment Squadron (B-52G)

5th Bombardment Wing (Heavy)

Travis AFB, California (1959–1968)

Minot AFB, North Dakota, (1968–present)

B-52B, 1959; B-52G, 1959-1968; B-52H, 1968-present

23rd Bombardment Squadron

31st Bombardment Squadron

72nd Bombardment Squadron (B-52H)

6th Bombardment (later Strategic Aerospace) Wing

Walker AFB, New Mexico

B-52E, 1957–1967

24th Bombardment Squadron

39th Bombardment Squadron

40th Bombardment Squadron

4129th Combat Crew Training Squadron (1959–1963)

7th Bombardment Wing (Heavy)

Carswell AFB, Texas

B-52F, 1958–1969; B-52D, 1969–1983; B-52H, 1982–1992

9th Bombardment Squadron

20th Bombardment Squadron (to 2nd BW 12/92)

11th Bombardment (later Strategic Aerospace) Wing

Altus AFB, Oklahoma

B-52E, 1958–1968

26th Bombardment Squadron

42nd Bombardment Squadron

17th Bombardment Wing (Heavy)
Wright-Patterson AFB, Ohio (1963-1975)
Beale AFB, California, (1975-1976)
(Superseded 4043rd Strategic Wing)
B-52E, 1963–1968; B-52H, 1968–1975; B-52G, 1975–1976
34th Bombardment Squadron

19th Bombardment Wing (Heavy)
Homestead AFB, Florida (1962–1968)
Robins AFB, Georgia (1968–1983)
B-52H, 1962–1968; B-52G, 1968–1983
28th Bombardment Squadron

22nd Bombardment Wing (Heavy)
March AFB, California
B-52B, 1963–1966; B-52D, 1966–1982
2nd Bombardment Squadron
486th Bombardment Squadron

28th Bombardment Wing (Heavy)
Ellsworth AFB, South Dakota
B-52D, 1957–1971; B-52G, 1971–1985
77th Bombardment Squadron
717th Bombardment Squadron
718th Bombardment Squadron

39th Bombardment Wing (Heavy)
Eglin AFB, Florida
(Superseded 4135th Strategic Wing)
B-52G, 1963-1965
62nd Bombardment Squadron

40th Air Expeditionary Wing
Diego Garcia, British Indian Ocean Territory
B-52H, 2001–c.2006
40th Expeditionary Bombardment Squadron

42nd Bombardment Wing (Heavy)
Loring AFB, Maine
B-52C, 1956–1957; B-52D, 1957–1959; B-52G, 1959–1994
69th Bombardment Squadron
70th Bombardment Squadron
75th Bombardment Squadron

43rd Strategic Wing
Andersen AFB, Guam
B-52D, 1972–1983; B-52G, 1983–1990
60th Bombardment Squadron
63rd Bombardment Squadron (Provisional), 1972–1973

68th Bombardment Wing (Heavy)
Seymour Johnson AFB, NC
(Superseded 4241st Strategic Wing)
B-52G, 1963–1982
51st Bombardment Squadron

70th Bombardment Wing (Heavy)
Clinton-Sherman AFB, Oklahoma
(Superseded 4123rd Strategic Wing)
B-52E, 1963–1968; B-52D, 1968–1969
6th Bombardment Squadron

72nd Bombardment Wing (Heavy)
Ramey AFB, Puerto Rico (1959–1971)
Andersen AFB, Guam (Provisional wing 1972–1973)
B-52G, 1959–1971, 1972–1973
60th Bombardment Squadron

91st Bombardment Wing (Heavy)
Glasgow AFB, Montana
(Superseded 4141st Strategic Wing)
B-52D, 1963–1968
322nd Bombardment Squadron

92nd Bombardment (later Strategic Aerospace) Wing
Fairchild AFB, Washington
B-52D, 1957–1971; B-52G, 1970–1986; B-52H, 1986–1994
325th Bombardment Squadron
326th Bombardment Squadron (B-52D)
327th Bombardment Squadron (B-52D)

93rd Bombardment Wing (Heavy)
Castle AFB, California
B-52B, 1955–1965; B-52D, 1956–1958; B-52E, 1957–1958, 1967–1970; B-52F, 1958–1974; B-52G, 1966–1967, 1974–1994; B-52H, 1974–1993
328th Bombardment Squadron
329th Bombardment Squadron
330th Bombardment Squadron (1955–1963) (1998–1991)
4017th Combat Crew Training Squadron (1955–1956)

95th Bombardment Wing (Heavy)
Biggs AFB, Texas
B-52B, 1959–1966
334th Bombardment Squadron (1959–1966)

96th Strategic Aerospace Wing

Dyess AFB, Texas

B-52E, 1963–1970; B-52D, 1969–1972; B-52H, 1982-1993

337th Bombardment Squadron

97th Bombardment Wing (Heavy)

Eaker AFB, Arkansas

B-52G, 1960–1992

340th Bombardment Squadron

99th Bombardment Wing (Heavy)

Westover AFB, Massachusetts

B-52C, 1956–1966; B-52B, 1958–1959; B-52D, 1957–1961, 1966–1974

346th Bombardment Squadron

347th Bombardment Squadron

348th Bombardment Squadron

306th Bombardment Wing (Heavy)

McCoy AFB, Florida

(Superseded 4047th Strategic Wing)

B-52D, 1963–1973

367th Bombardment Squadron

307th Strategic Wing

U-Tapao RTNAF, Thailand

B-52D, 1973–1975

364th Bombardment Squadron (Provisional)

365th Bombardment Squadron (Provisional)

307th Bombardment Wing (Air Force Reserve Command)

Barksdale AFB, Louisiana

B-52H, 1993–present

93rd Bombardment Squadron

343rd Bombardment Squadron

319th Bombardment Wing (Heavy)

Grand Forks AFB, North Dakota

(Superseded 4133rd Strategic Wing)

B-52H, 1963–1982; B-52G, 1982–1987

46th Bombardment Squadron

320th Bombardment Wing (Heavy)

Mather AFB, California

(Superseded 4134th Strategic Wing)

B-52F, 1963–1968; B-52G, 1968–1989

441st Bombardment Squadron

340th Bombardment Wing (Heavy)

Bergstrom AFB, Texas

(Superseded 4130th Strategic Wing)

B-52D, 1963–1966

486th Bombardment Squadron

366th Wing

(Headquartered at Mountain Home AFB, Idaho; aircraft located at Castle AFB, California)

B-52G, 1992–1994

34th Bombardment Squadron

376th Strategic Wing

Kadena AB, Okinawa

4180th Bombardment Squadron (Provisional) (never operational)

379th Bombardment Wing (Heavy)

Wurtsmith AFB, Michigan

B-52H, 1961–1977; B-52G, 1977–1992

524th Bombardment Squadron

380th Strategic Aerospace Wing

Plattsburgh AFB, New York

B-52G, 1966–1971

528th Bombardment Squadron

397th Bombardment Wing (Heavy)

Dow AFB, Maine

(Superseded 4038th Strategic Wing)

B-52G, 1963–1968

596th Bombardment Squadron

410th Bombardment Wing (Heavy)

K. I. Sawyer AFB, Michigan

(Superseded 4042nd Strategic Wing)

B-52H, 1963–1994

644th Bombardment Squadron

416th Bombardment Wing (Heavy)

Griffiss AFB, New York

(Superseded 4039th Strategic Wing)

B-52G, 1963–1992; B-52H, 1992–1995

668th Bombardment Squadron

449th Bombardment Wing (Heavy)

Kincheloe AFB, Michigan

(Superseded 4239th Strategic Wing)

B-52H, 1963–1977

716th Bombardment Squadron

450th Bombardment Wing (Heavy)
Minot AFB, North Dakota
(Superseded 4136th Strategic Wing)
B-52H, 1963–1968
720th Bombardment Squadron

454th Bombardment Wing (Heavy)
Columbus AFB, Mississippi
(Superseded 4228th Strategic Wing)
B-52F, 1963–1966; B-52D, 1966–1969
736th Bombardment Squadron

456th Strategic Aerospace (later Bombardment) Wing
Beale AFB, California
(superseded 4126th Strategic Wing)
B-52G, 1963–1975
744th Bombardment Squadron

461st Bombardment Wing (Heavy)
Amarillo AFB, Texas
(superseded 4128th Strategic Wing)
B-52D, 1963–1968
764th Bombardment Squadron
462nd Strategic Aerospace Wing
Larson AFB, Washington
(Superseded 4170th Strategic Wing)
B-52D, 1963–1966
768th Bombardment Squadron

465th Bombardment Wing (Heavy)
Robins AFB, Georgia
(Superseded 4137th Strategic Wing)
B-52G, 1963–1968
781st Bombardment Squadron

484th Bombardment Wing (Heavy)
Turner AFB, Georgia
(Superseded 4138th Strategic Wing)
B-52D, 1963–1967
824th Bombardment Squadron

494th Bombardment Wing (Heavy)
Sheppard AFB, Texas
(Superseded 4245th Strategic Wing)
B-52D, 1963–1966
864th Bombardment Squadron

509th Bombardment Wing (Heavy)
Pease AFB, New Hampshire
B-52D, 1966–1969
393rd Bombardment Squadron

806th Provisional Bombardment Wing
RAF Fairford, England
Activated for Operation Desert Shield/Desert Storm in January 1991. (Inactivated March 1991)
Composed of B-52G aircraft and personnel from the 62nd, 340th, 524th, and 668th Bombardment Squadrons

1701st Provisional Air Refueling Wing
Prince Abdulla AB, Jeddah, Saudi Arabia
Activated for Operation Desert Shield/Desert Storm in August 1990. (Inactivated March 1991)
Air refueling wing with 6 B-52Gs from 60th Bombardment Squadron (January–March 1991)

1703rd Provisional Air Refueling Wing
King Khalid Military City, Saudi Arabia
Activated for Operation Desert Shield/ Desert Storm in August 1990. (Inactivated March 1991)
Air refueling wing with 7 B-52Gs from 69th Bombardment Squadron (October 1990–March 1991)

1708th Provisional Bombardment Wing
Prince Abdulla AB, Jeddah, Saudi Arabia
Activated for Operation Desert Shield/Desert Storm in August 1990. (Inactivated March 1991)
Composed of B-52G aircraft and personnel from the 69th and 524th Bombardment Squadrons (August 1990–March 1991) Additional B-52G aircraft and personnel from the 69th, 524th, 596th, 328th and 668th Bombardment Squadrons (December 1990-March 1991)

4038th Strategic Wing
Dow AFB, Maine
B-52G, 1960–1963
341st Bombardment Squadron (Inactivated in 1963; and aircraft reassigned to the 596th Bombardment Squadron, 397th Bombardment Wing)

4039th Strategic Wing

Griffiss AFB, New York

B-52G, 1960–1963

75th Bombardment Squadron (Inactivated in 1963; and aircraft reassigned to the 668th Bombardment Squadron, 416th Bombardment Wing)

4042nd Strategic Wing

K. I. Sawyer AFB, Michigan

B-52H, 1961–1963

526th Bombardment Squadron (Inactivated in 1963; and aircraft reassigned to the 644th Bombardment Squadron, 410th Bombardment Wing)

4043rd Strategic Wing

Wright-Patterson AFB, Ohio

B-52E, 1960–1963

42nd Bombardment Squadron (Inactivated in 1963; and aircraft reassigned to the 34th Bombardment Squadron, 17th Bombardment Wing)

4047th Strategic Wing

McCoy AFB, Florida

B-52D, 1961–1963

347th Bombardment Squadron (Inactivated in 1963; and aircraft reassigned to the 367th Bombardment Squadron, 306th Bombardment Wing)

4123rd Strategic Wing

Clinton-Sherman AFB, Oklahoma

B-52E, 1959–1963

98th Bombardment Squadron (Inactivated in 1963; and aircraft reassigned to the 6th Bombardment Squadron, 70th Bombardment Wing)

4126th Strategic Wing

Beale AFB, California

B-52G, 1960–1963

31st Bombardment Squadron (Inactivated in 1963; and aircraft reassigned to the 744th Bombardment Squadron, 456th SAW)

4128th Strategic Wing

Amarillo AFB, Texas

B-52D, 1960–1963

718th Bombardment Squadron (Inactivated in 1963; and aircraft reassigned to the 764th Bombardment Squadron, 461st Bombardment Wing)

4130th Strategic Wing

Bergstrom AFB, Texas

B-52D, 1959–1963

335th Bombardment Squadron (Inactivated on 1 September 1963; and aircraft reassigned to the 486th Bombardment Squadron, 340th Bombardment Wing)

4133rd Strategic Wing

Grand Forks AFB, North Dakota

B-52H, 1962–1963

30th Bombardment Squadron (Inactivated in 1963; and aircraft reassigned to the 46th Bombardment Squadron, 319th Bombardment Wing)

4133rd Strategic Wing (Provisional)

Andersen AFB, Guam

Provisional Vietnam-era SAC unit, February 1966–July 1970

(Superseded by 43rd Strategic Wing)

4134th Strategic Wing

Mather AFB, California

B-52F, 1958–1963

72nd Bombardment Squadron (Inactivated on 1 September 1963; and aircraft reassigned to the 441st Bombardment Squadron, 320th BW)

4135th Strategic Wing

Eglin AFB, Florida

B-52G, 1959–1963

301st Bombardment Squadron (Inactivated in 1963; and aircraft reassigned to the 62nd Bombardment Squadron, 39th Bombardment Wing)

4136th Strategic Wing

Minot AFB, North Dakota

B-52H, 1961–1963

525th Bombardment Squadron (Inactivated in 1963; and aircraft reassigned to the 720th Bombardment Squadron, 450th Bombardment Wing)

4137th Strategic Wing

Robins AFB, Georgia

B-52G, 1960–1963

342nd Bombardment Squadron (Inactivated in 1963; and aircraft reassigned to the 781st Bombardment Squadron, 465th Bombardment Wing)

4138th Strategic Wing

Turner AFB, Georgia

B-52D, 1959–1963

336th Bombardment Squadron (Inactivated in 1963; and aircraft reassigned to the 824th Bombardment Squadron, 484th BW

4141st Strategic Wing

Glasgow AFB, Montana

B-52D, 1959–1963

326th Bombardment Squadron (Inactivated in 1963; and aircraft reassigned to the 322nd Bombardment Squadron, 91st Bombardment Wing)

4170th Strategic Wing

Larson AFB, Washington

B-52D, 1960–1963

327th Bombardment Squadron (Inactivated in 1963; and aircraft reassigned to the 768th Bombardment Squadron, 462nd Bombardment Wing)

4228th Strategic Wing

Columbus AFB, Mississippi

B-52F, 1959–1963

492nd Bombardment Squadron (Inactivated in 1963; and aircraft reassigned to the 736th Bombardment Squadron, 454th Bombardment Wing)

4238th Strategic Wing

Barksdale AFB, Louisiana

B-52F, 1958–1963

436th Bombardment Squadron (Inactivated in 1963; and aircraft reassigned to the 20th Bombardment Squadron, 2nd Bombardment Wing)

4239th Strategic Wing

Kincheloe AFB, Michigan

B-52H, 1961–1963

93rd Bombardment Squadron (Inactivated in 1963; and aircraft reassigned to the 716th Bombardment Squadron, 449th Bombardment Wing)

4241st Strategic Wing

Seymour Johnson AFB, North Carolina

B-52G, 1959–1963

73rd Bombardment Squadron (Inactivated in 1963; and aircraft reassigned to the 51st Bombardment Squadron, 68th Bombardment Wing)

4245th Strategic Wing

Sheppard AFB, Texas

B-52D, 1960–1963

717th Bombardment Squadron (Inactivated in 1963; and aircraft reassigned to the 864th Bombardment Squadron, 494th Bombardment Wing)

4252nd Strategic Wing (Provisional)

Kadena AB, Okinawa

Provisional Vietnam-era SAC unit, April 1967– April 1970

(Superseded by 376th Strategic Wing)

4258th Strategic Wing (Provisional)

U-Tapao RTNAF, Thailand

Provisional Vietnam-era SAC unit, April 1967– April 1970

(Superseded by 307th Strategic Wing)

Equipped primarily with B-52D aircraft; aircrew and support personnel deployed from stateside B-52 wings on a rotational basis

4300th Provisional Bombardment Wing

Diego Garcia AB, British Indian Ocean Territories

Activated for Operation Desert Shield/ Desert Storm in January 1991. (Inactivated March 1991)

Composed of B-52G aircraft and personnel from the 69th and 328th Bombardment Squadrons

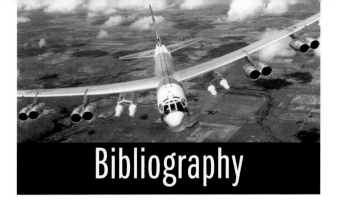

Bibliography

Activity Input to Project Corona Harvest, Arc Light. Offutt AFB, Nebraska: SAC/History Office, 1970.

Andrade, John. *U.S. Military Aircraft Designations and Serials since 1909*. Hinckley, UK: Midland Counties Publications, 1979.

B-52G Desert Storm Bombing Survey. Offutt AFB, Nebraska: Strategic Air Command, 1991.

B-52 Propulsion Capability Study. Wright-Patterson AFB, Ohio: ACSSW/PRSS, 2005.

Boeing Historical Archives. *Pedigree of Champions: Boeing since 1916*. 6th ed. Seattle, Wash.: Boeing Historical Archives, 1985.

Bowers, Peter M., and Gordon Swanborough. *United States Military Aircraft Since 1909*. Washington, DC: Smithsonian Institution Press, 1989.

Bowers, Peter M. *Boeing Aircraft Since 1916*. Annapolis: Naval Institute Press, 1989.

———. *Boeing B-52A/H Stratofortress. Aircraft in Profile, Volume 13*. Windsor, Berkshire, UK: Profile Publications Ltd., 1973.

Boyne, Walter. *Boeing B-52: A Documentary History*. Washington, DC: Smithsonian Institution Press, 1981.

Budiansky, Stephen. *Air Power: The Men, Machines, and Ideas that Revolutionized War, from Kitty Hawk to Iraq*. New York: Penguin Books, 2004.

Bulletin of the Atomic Scientists. Thousand Oaks, Calif.: SAGE Publications USA, published continuously since 1945.

Burris, P.M., and M. A. Bender. *Aircraft Load Alleviation and Mode Stabilization (LAMS): B-52 System Analysis, Synthesis, and Design*. Wichita: Boeing Wichita, 1969.

Clodfelter, Mark. *The Limits of Air Power: The American Bombing of North Vietnam*. New York: Free Press, 1989.

Condor, Albert E. *Air Force Gunners (AFGA): The Men Behind the Guns, The History of Enlisted Aerial Gunnery, 1917–1991*. Nashville, Tennessee: Turner Publishing, 1994.

Cooke, David C. *How Airplanes are Made*. New York: Dodd, Mead & Company, 1956.

Cordesman, Anthony H., and Abraham R. Wagner. *The Lessons of Modern War: The Gulf War*. Boulder, Colo.: Westview Press, 1996.

Davis, Larry. *B-52 Stratofortress in Action*. Carrollton, Tex.: Squadron/Signal Publications, 1992.

Desert Storm After Action Report (S/NF). MacDill Air Force Base, Fla.: CENTCOM, 1991.

Dick, Ron, and Dan Patterson. *Aviation Century: War & Peace In The Air*. Eden Prairie, Ontario: Boston Mills Press, 2006.

Donald, David. *The Encyclopedia of World Aircraft*. Etobicoke, Ontario, Canada: Prospero Books, 1997.

Dorr, Robert F. "Stratofortress: The Big One from Boeing." *Air Enthusiast*, No. 41, Midsummer 1990. Bromley, Kent, UK: Pilot Press, 1990.

Dorr, Robert F., and Brian C. Rogers. "Boeing B-52H: The Ultimate Warrior." *World Air Power Journal*, Volume 27, Winter 1996. London: Aerospace Publishing.

Dorr, Robert F., and Lindsay Peacock. *Boeing's Cold War Warrior: B-52 Stratofortress*. London: Osprey Aerospace, 1995.

Drendel, Lou. *B-52 Stratofortress in Action*. Carrollton, Tex.: Squadron/Signal Publications, 1975.

Eden, Paul, ed. "Boeing B-52 Stratofortress." *Encyclopedia of Modern Military Aircraft*. London: Amber Books, 2004.

Ethell, Jeffrey L. *B-52 Stratofortress*. London: Arms and Armour Press, 1989.

Final Report to Congress: Conduct of the Persian Gulf War. Washington, DC: Department of Defense, 1992.

Flinn, Kelly J. *Proud to Be: My Life, The Air Force, The Controversy*. New York: Random House, 1997.

Futrell, R. F., et al. *The United States Air Force in Southeast Asia: Aces and Aerial victories, 1965–1973*. Washington, DC: Office of Air Force History, 1976.

Futrell, Robert Frank. *Ideas, Concepts, Doctrine. Vol. 2, Basic Thinking in the United States Air Force, 1907–1984*. Maxwell AFB, Ala.: Air University Press, 1989.

Gravel, Mike, ed. *Pentagon Papers: Department of Defense History of United States Decision Making in Vietnam*. 4 vols. Boston: Beacon Press, 1971.

Greenwood, John T., ed. *Milestones of Aviation*. Washington, DC: Smithsonian Institute NASM, 1995.

Gunston, Bill. "Boeing B-52:The Strategic Stratofortress." *Flight*, Vol. 72, No. 2547, 15 November 1957.

Head, William P. *War From Above The Clouds: B-52 Operations during the Second Indochina War and the Effects of the Air War on Theory and Doctrine*. Maxwell AFB, Ala.: Air University Press, 2002.

History of the Strategic Air Command 1946-1981. Offutt AFB, Nebraska: Office of the Historian, Strategic Air Command, 1982.

History of the Strategic Air Command 1 Jan - 31 Dec 1990. Offutt AFB, Nebraska: Office of the Historian, Strategic Air Command, 1992.

Hosmer, Stephen T. *The Conflict Over Kosovo: Why Milosevic Decided to Settle When He Did*. Santa Monica: RAND, 2000.

Improving the Efficiency of Engines for Large Nonfighter Aircraft. Maxwell AFB, Ala.: Air Force Studies Board, 2007.

Jenkins, Dennis R. *B-1 Lancer: The Most Complicated Warplane Ever Developed*. New York: McGraw-Hill, 1999.

Johnston, Alvin "Tex," with Charles Barton. *Jet-Age Test Pilot*. Washington, DC: Smithsonian, 1984.

Keaney, Thomas A., and Eliot A. Cohen. *Gulf War Air Power Survey, Summary Report*. Washington, DC: U.S. Air Force, 1993.

Knaack, Marcelle Size. *Encyclopedia of U.S. Air Force Aircraft and Missile Systems. Vol. 2, Post-World War II Bombers, 1945–1973*. Washington, DC: Air Force History Office, 1988.

———. *Post-World War II Bombers, 1945-1973*. Washington, D.C.: Office of Air Force History, 1988.

Kohn, Richard H., and Joseph P. Harahan, eds. *Air Superiority in World War II and Korea: An Interview with Gen. James Ferguson, Gen. Robert M. Lee, Gen. William Momyer, and Lt. Gen. Elwood R. Quesada*. Washington, DC: Air Force History Office, 1983.

Kopp, Dr. Carlo. *Operation Enduring Freedom Analysis*. Online: Air Power Australia Analyses, 2002.

Kutler, Stanley, ed. *Encyclopedia of the Vietnam War*. New York: Charles Scribner's Sons, 1996.

Lake, Jon, and Mark Styling. *B-52 Stratofortress Units in Combat 1955-73*. London: Osprey Publishing, 2004.

Lake, Jon. *B-52 Stratofortress Units in Operation Desert Storm*. London: Osprey Publishing, 2004.

———. "Variant Briefing: Boeing B-52 Stratofortress: Part 1". *International Air Power Review*, Volume Eight, Spring 2003. Norwalk, Conn.: AIRtime Publishing, 2003.

———. "Variant Briefing: Boeing B-52 Stratofortress: Part 2". *International Air Power Review*, Volume Nine, Summer 2003. Norwalk, Conn.: AIRtime Publishing, 2003.

Lambeth, Benjamin S. *Air Power Against Terror: America's Conduct of Operation Enduring Freedom*. Santa Monica: RAND Corporation (MG-166-1), 2005

———. *NATO's Air War For Kosovo: A Strategic and Operational Assessment*. Santa Monica: RAND, 2001

LeMay, Curtis E. "Air Power in Guerrilla Warfare." *Air Force Information Policy Letter for Commanders*. Washington, DC: Office of the Secretary of the Air Force, 15 April 1962.

LeMay, Curtis E., and MacKinlay Kantor. *Mission with LeMay: My Story*. New York: Doubleday and Co., 1965.

LeMay, Curtis E., with Bill Yenne. *Superfortress: The B-29 and American Air Power*. New York: McGraw Hill, 1988; Yardley, Pennsylvania: Westholme, 2006.

Lloyd, Alwyn T. *B-52 Stratofortress in Detail and Scale, Volume 27*. Blue Ridge Summit, Pa.: Tab Books Inc., 1988.

Maier, Lothar Nick. *BUFF: Big Ugly Fat F******. Bloomington, Ind.: Trafford Publishing, 2002.

Marshall, L. Michel. *The Eleven Days of Christmas: America's Last Vietnam Battle*. San Francisco: Encounter Books, 2002.

McCarthy, Donald J. Jr. *MiG Killers: A Chronology of U.S. Air Victories in Vietnam 1965–1973*. North Branch, Minn.: Specialty Press, 2009.

McCarthy, James R. and George B. Allison. *Linebacker II: A View From the Rock*. Maxwell AFB, Alabama: Airpower Research Institute, Air War College, 1979.

Momyer, General William W. *Air Power in Three Wars*. Washington, DC: GPO, 1978.

Morrocco, John. *Rain of Fire: Air War, 1969–1973*. Vietnam Experience Series, Ed. Robert Manning. Boston: Boston Publishing Co., 1986.

Nalty, Bernard C. *Air War Over South Vietnam, 1968–1975*. Anacostia, DC: Air Force Historical Studies Office.

Nixon, Richard M. *In the Arena: A Memoir of Victory, Defeat, and Renewal*. New York: Simon & Schuster, 1990.

———. *RN: The Memoirs of Richard Nixon*. 2 vols. New York: Warner Books, 1978.

Palmer, Bruce, ed. *Grand Strategy for the 1980s*. Washington, DC: American Enterprises Institute for Public Policy Research, 1978.

Redding, Robert, and Bill Yenne. *Boeing: Planemaker to the World*. New York: Crown Publishers, 1983.

Schlight, John. *The Air War in South Vietnam: The Years of the Offensive, 1965–1968*. Washington, DC: Air Force History Office, 1988.

Tagg, Lori S. *Development of the B-52: The Wright Field Story*. Dayton, Ohio: History Office Aeronautical Systems Center, Air Force Materiel Command, Wright-Patterson Air Force Base, United States Air Force, 2004.

Technology Options for Improved Air Vehicle Fuel Efficiency. Maxwell AFB, Ala.: Air Force Scientific Advisory Board, 2006.

Tillman, Barrett. *LeMay*. New York: Palgrave Macmillan, 2007.

Tretler, Col. David, Lt. Col. Daniel T. Kuehl, Col. Emery M. Kiraly, Lt. Col. Robert C. Owen, and Dr. Aron Pinker. *Gulf War Air Power Survey, Chronology of the Gulf War*. Washington, DC: U.S. Air Force, 1993.

Truong, Nhu Tang. *A Vietcong Memoir: An Inside Account of the Vietnam War and Its Aftermath*. New York: Harcourt Brace and Jovanovich, 1985.

Undersecretary of Defense for Acquisition, Technology, and Logistics. *Task Force on B-52H Re-engining (Revised and Updated)*. Washington, DC: Department of Defense, 2004.

U.S. Department of Defense. *Soviet Military Power*. Washington, DC: U.S. Government Printing Office, various editions, 1981–1987.

Van Staaveren, Jacob. *Gradual Failure: the Air War Over North Vietnam, 1965–1966*. Anacostia, DC: Air Force Historical Studies Office, 2002.

Wagner, Ray. American Combat Planes, Third Enlarged Edition. New York: Doubleday, 1982.

Willis, David. "Boeing's Timeless Deterrent, Part 1: B-52 Stratofortress: From Conception to Hanoi." *Air Enthusiast*, No. 119, September/October 2005. Stamford, Lincs, UK: Key Publishing, 2005.

———. "Boeing's Timeless Deterrent, Part 2: B-52: The Permanent Spear Tip." *Air Enthusiast*, No. 120, November/December 2005. Stamford, Lincs, UK: Key Publishing, 2005.

Winchester, Jim, ed. "Boeing B-52 Stratofortress (SAC)." *Military Aircraft of the Cold War (The Aviation Factfile)*. London: Grange Books plc, 2006.

Yenne, Bill. *SAC, A Primer of Modern Strategic Airpower*. Novato: Presidio Press, 1985.

———. *The History of the U.S. Air Force*. New York: Simon & Schuster, Exeter Books, 1984.

———. *The Story of the Boeing Company*. Minneapolis: Zenith, 2010.

Index

▓ Next page: A B-52H of the 419th Flight Test Squadron flies over a snow-covered Alaskan mountain range at 75 degrees north latitude, close to the North Pole, during an Avionics Mid-life Improvement test mission. *USAF photo, Sgt. Brian Schlumbohm*